Learning Communities 2.0

Educating in the
Age of Empowerment

William G. Spady and Charles J. Schwahn

Published in partnership with the
American Association of School Administrators

ROWMAN & LITTLEFIELD EDUCATION
A division of
ROWMAN & LITTLEFIELD PUBLISHERS, INC.
Lanham • New York • Toronto • Plymouth, UK

Published in partnership with the American Association of School Administrators

Published by Rowman & Littlefield Education
A division of Rowman & Littlefield Publishers, Inc.
A wholly owned subsidiary of The Rowman & Littlefield Publishing Group, Inc.
4501 Forbes Boulevard, Suite 200, Lanham, Maryland 20706
http://www.rowmaneducation.com

Estover Road, Plymouth PL6 7PY, United Kingdom

British Library Cataloguing in Publication Information Available

Library of Congress Cataloging-in-Publication Data

Spady, William G.
  Learning communities 2.0 : educating in the age of empowerment / William G. Spady and Charles J. Schwahn.
      p. cm.
  "Published in partnership with the American Association of School Administrators."
  ISBN 978-1-60709-606-1 (cloth : alk. paper) — ISBN 978-1-60709-607-8 (pbk. : alk. paper) — ISBN 978-1-60709-608-5 (electronic)
  1. School improvement programs—United States. 2. Educational leadership—United States. 3. Professional learning communities—United States. 4. Educational change—United States. I. Spady, William G. II. American Association of School Administrators. III. Title.
  LB2822.82.S387 2010
  371.2'07—dc22   2009050479

∞™ The paper used in this publication meets the minimum requirements of American National Standard for Information Sciences—Permanence of Paper for Printed Library Materials, ANSI/NISO Z39.48-1992.

Printed in the United States of America

CONTENTS

PREFACE

> If they give you this much space
>
> ⧠
>
> to record a student's learning,
> they sure must not want to know much!

Can the message be clearer? For a century American education—like the other education systems in the modern world—has been caught in a grand illusion. And generations of its constituents and practitioners have been told, and forced to believe, that this illusion is reality. Well, in fact, it's a reality that we've created to convince ourselves that numbers placed in boxes are our learning, our potential, our achievement, our worth, and our passport to the future. And today this illusionary reality has become not only a powerful force in shaping our cultural thinking, it's become the law of the land—whether you call it No Child Left Behind, national standards, accountability, or Race to the Top.

This illusion is the product of, and fully embodies, a closed-system paradigm we call "educentrism." Educentrism approaches and implements change from inside the framework of how the education system itself is already structured. It simply assumes that things like grade levels, semesters, subject areas, grading periods, school years, self-contained classrooms, and so on, both exist and must continue to exist. Therefore, both reform thinking and change efforts must occur within these organizational/institutionalized constructs and constraints. We address the artificiality and profound limitations of educentrism right off the bat in chapter 1 and offer tangible alternatives to each of its entrenched features from that point forward.

Hence, for us, this book and others like it symbolize a revolution of sorts—a Declaration of Human Empowerment for those who choose to endorse and embrace it:

> Human beings, their learning, their potential, their achievement, their worth, and their passports to the future *cannot* and *will not* be reduced to a few numbers in tiny boxes that "reformers," ideologues, and politicians can hold up to either praise or ridicule!

The essence of our argument is in chapter 3, and if its five key knowledge bases that underlie empowering learning don't convince you of the misguided and superficial nature of today's educentric "reform" efforts, perhaps nothing will.

But please don't misinterpret our intent. We've focused this book on the positive, not the negative—what real people can do to create something far more meaningful and impactful than what we've known since the nineteenth century as "school in a box." It represents nearly a hundred years of our combined experience in education—as teachers, scholars, leaders, and international consultants—and decades of devoted study to what learning is, the depth of human capacity and potential, how effective learning systems function, what effective leaders do to achieve productive change, how the future is unfolding, what modern technologies can contribute to learning systems, and what empowerment means to humanity's future.

As Chuck likes to say: "To steal from one is plagiarism, but to steal from many is research." And boy, have we been researching all of the above!

As a consequence, we take little credit for being original thinkers or educational pioneers. Those credits go to legendary figures like Rudolph Steiner, John Dewey, and Maria Montessori. We've simply done our best to synthesize their work and all of this other knowledge into a framework and implementation strategy that people can work with effectively.

The result of our efforts is a process we call strategic design and a model that we call an empowering learning community (ELC). We've done our best here to capture the essence of an ELC in five systemic components:

1. Its collegial culture of professionalism (chapter 2)

2. Its transformational philosophy and rationale (chapter 3)

3. Its life-performance learner outcomes (chapter 4)

4. Its empowering learning system (chapters 5 and 6)

5. Its aligned support structure (chapter 7)

Try as we might, we couldn't legitimately reduce the defining elements of a learning community to fewer than these five essential components, and we've done our best to bring each to light with examples from the "real world" that are both powerful and persuasive.

Nonetheless, we harbor no illusions about this book. The challenge it represents in the face of today's quantitatively obsessed educentric reform juggernaut is daunting. And it requires real leadership to pull off—the kind described in detail in its companion book *Total Leaders 2.0*. We view the two books as an integrated whole, since both use today's emerging age of empowerment as the "real" reality we all face and for which we're being challenged to educate our young people. Moreover, we hope that you find unique insights and valuable resources in both books and that you will use them as the basis for your own Declaration of Human Empowerment. That alone will have made our decades of work and the crafting of these two books worth the effort.

Bill Spady
Chuck Schwahn

TRANSFORMATIONAL CHANGE: FROM EDUCENTRISM TO EMPOWERING LEARNING COMMUNITIES

We've been champions of change since each of our careers in education began well over forty years ago, and we haven't lost an ounce of our drive over that long period. In fact, our convictions about educational change, and our accumulated experience and knowledge about it, have only intensified in the past decade or so. Why? Because our work has always been future focused, and we really pay close attention to what's happening in the world that will affect the environment in which organizations and their people operate.

Given this forward-looking outlook, we believe that our world has recently undergone yet another exciting evolutionary step forward to what we called and described in *Total Leaders 2.0* as the "age of empowerment." And that step has made it even more urgent than ever for education to catch up—to get future focused, learner centered, and to fundamentally change.

Today's Age of Empowerment

For us the age of empowerment represents a major step beyond what people have been calling the information age, and a giant leap beyond the industrial age that so completely dominated most of the twentieth century. We summarized the "good news" about this evolution in chapter 1 of *TL2.0*, and the prevailing concerns about it in chapter 2. We called it Empowermentland just to emphasize the point, and we recommend that you read both chapters if you want a deeper understanding of our thinking about the world we're living in today.

The essence of the empowerment age message is that people in today's world have more knowledge, opportunities, choices, capacity to communicate, and support systems available to them than ever before in history—and more than one could have imagined just a couple of decades ago. This literal explosion of opportunities and options is largely a result of the transformational technologies that have emerged in the past decade—technologies that have changed how we live, learn, and lead. And it's accompanied by a small but rapidly expanding movement in human consciousness; that is, people are seeing themselves as having far greater inner power and potential than their societies/cultures have assumed and/or allowed them to develop and express in the past, and they're acting on those expanded realizations.

When you translate these two major shifts into an educational context, it reveals that:

> Anyone can learn anything at anytime from anywhere from world-class experts using the most transformational technologies and resources available to enhance their personal interests and life fulfillment.

Please read that again, because it represents an incredibly empowering set of conditions, and it will serve as the bedrock for everything else that follows in this chapter and this book.

The institution called "education" faces a huge dilemma in light of these conditions: It's fundamentally a product and the lingering embodiment of century-old industrial age beliefs, reasoning, priorities, and operations. And its purposes, policies, legal and regulatory constraints, operating structures, and prevalent practices are deeply entrenched. The consequence of these two factors is what we call its all-pervasive "assembly-line" instructional system.

Our increased sense of urgency about educational change, then, directly reflects what we see as the ever-widening gap between the age of empowerment's social, political, technological, and learning "realities" on the one hand, and education's static, industrial age status on the other. One is moving rapidly in the direction of expanding opportunity and empowerment, and the other is being forced—through "reform" policy mandates—either to stay right where it is, or actually move in the other direction: toward even more standardization and constraint, and less choice.

To support our point, please consider the following characterization of the pattern that embodies both the system's industrial age practices and the reform mandates that are reinforcing them:

Specific students of a specific age must learn specific things on a specific schedule in a specific classroom from a specific teacher using specific materials and methods so that they can pass specific tests on specific dates—and only then will they specifically be called "OK."

Please read this again and take a minute to really let it sink in. To us this pattern is both emotionally and intellectually distressing. It is mechanistic, rigid, and insensitive to both those who teach and those who are there to learn. And it's counterproductive. In its attempt to equalize opportunity by giving everyone exactly the same amount of time to learn and do things at the same time and on the same schedule, it is actually creating the conditions that produce what the system calls "failure." Because if you can't do it in the time allowed, you lose!

And please understand, when we first asserted this piece of insight nearly twenty years ago, it was only two lines long. It used to end with the word "teacher." We've felt compelled to add the last two lines since the emergence of the standards and accountability movement in the past decade. And, yes, we're going to say it: The pattern's only gotten more rigid under the federal No Child Left Behind initiative and its state-based testing cousins. Consequently, today's schools, educators, and students are "boxed in" tighter than anyone can remember—and we say this with great empathy. Most of the humans who are in these boxes/constraints don't like them at all, and we want you to join us in changing them. No, not just change them—transform them!

Not All Change Is Created Equal

We're inviting you here to go with us on a journey that will take us from "education in a box" to a very different place—almost as different as the two descriptions above. It's called an empowering learning community, and in it you'll find very few, if any, constraining boxes of any consequence. To get there you have a choice. You can walk the path of change, starting from where you are and moving forward. Or you can fly on a magic carpet of sorts using a process called "creation," where you simply start over by creating what you really want without the constraints of the past. In both cases we're seeking something called "transformation," and that's a pretty tall order. So here are some guideposts to orient you along the way.

The Critical Pillars of Change

Regardless of which route you take, change or creation, you're going to be encountering inevitable challenges to where you're going, and that's going to require a lot of leadership insight and skill. That's why it would be wise for you to really study what's in *Total Leaders 2.0*—because it offers a wealth of insights about what it means to lead change of any kind, large or small. And it provides constant reminders of why there are so many obstacles on your path, most of them being the wreckage of failed change efforts from the past.

We think that most of that wreckage is there because the leaders of those well-meaning efforts didn't adequately establish what we call the "pillars of change." As their name implies, they literally hold up/bolster/support any kind of change effort. Based on the enormous body of research and experience on which they're based, we think that with them you've got a very good chance of succeeding. But without them you'd be wise to set your cell phone to auto-dial 911. Here they are—memorize and use them:

- **Purpose**. The deep and compelling reason an entity/organization exists. It embodies the organization's ends, defines its intended results, establishes the "meaning" that activities have, and clarifies what it is ultimately there to accomplish. Without it, participants lack focus, direction, priorities, and the reason for doing anything—change included.

- **Vision**. A clear, detailed picture of what your organization will be doing when operating at its ideal best to accomplish its purpose. This ideal describes the very best job you could possibly do based on your highest aspirations and deepest motivations. It's your "roadmap to success." Without it your people won't have a clear picture of the change you seek to make.

- **Ownership**. The emotional and motivational investment your personnel make in fully implementing your organization's vision and accomplishing its purpose. It results from involving everyone in the purpose-defining and vision-framing processes. Without their involvement, they'll lack the commitment to implement the changes implied in the purpose and vision— "Too different; too much hard work."

- **Capacity**. Having the knowledge, skills, abilities, and tools to get the job done well—with expertise, facility, and quality. That job is fully implementing the organization's vision and accomplishing its purpose. It can't be short-changed or overlooked because it embodies your people's ability to actually execute/do/implement what the purpose and vision require. Without it, practice spelling "train-wreck."

- **Support**. The direct, tangible assistance that your organization provides to its members to make the change happen successfully. That means organizing job responsibilities, schedules, time, compensation, physical arrangements, space, technologies, information flow, performance results, and technical assistance. Without adequate support, people simply lack the opportunity to shape and make the desired change.

These five pillars are a critical component of the Total Leaders model, and we strongly recommend that you make them a central part of how you approach any change effort, large or small. And don't forget our point about 911.

The Many Levels of Change

Our second piece of advice to assist you in your transformational journey is to look critically at what people claim is significant educational change. Most of it isn't. Instead, it's rather narrow, shallow, and inside the box. We learned this the hard way over decades of searching for compelling examples of future-focused, deeply empowering education in the public sector. So as you proceed, we encourage you to look insightfully at the educational change efforts you encounter, and keep a sharp eye out for the following:

1. We've encountered mountains of studies that describe what we came to call "cosmetic change," where things generally get relabeled and repackaged, but at the core, educational practice remains virtually the same as before. They're what we also call "technical tinkering."

2. There's also a lot of "procedural change" research out there. It involves people doing some things a bit differently than before, and on a different schedule. But it too doesn't get close to what "deeply empowering" really means.

3. Deeper still is a host of things we eventually named "programmatic change"—modifying and moving segments of the existing curriculum around and sometimes making them available to more/different students than before. But it rarely reflects what we know either "future focused" or "deeply empowering" means.

4. Nor do the host of things we eventually called "technical change," whether reflected in improved teaching skills or in using computers more extensively in classrooms. We applaud both, but they too don't hit the mark.

5. There are also innovations purported to represent "structural change," but they mainly involve two kinds of things: (1) playing with open space and team teaching configurations, or (2) juggling various combinations of grade levels into different buildings and calling them things like junior primary, middle school, and so on. Closer, but still "No cigar."

6. There's also a lot of work out there focused on "cultural change." It looks more deeply at patterns of values, expectations, relationships, and interpersonal dynamics involving both staff and students. Its first cousin relates to "school climate."

They're both important in understanding and achieving deeply empowering change, but they're only part of the picture.

7. Of particular interest are change efforts that claim to be "systemic"—which sure seems to imply being deep and comprehensive. But alas, most of them are mostly combinations of cosmetic, procedural, programmatic, technical, structural, and cultural changes that are simply being implemented "system-wide" in entire school districts—without impacting the nature of education as a system at all.

Enter Paradigmatic Change

Dissatisfied with what we had seen over many years of study, we felt compelled to forge our own definition of the kind of deep change that was implied in being genuinely future focused and empowering. And we did so with the indirect help of the brilliant futurist Joel Barker and his widely viewed 1988 video *Discovering the Future: The Business of Paradigms.* In it Barker lucidly illustrates what a paradigm is and how deeply it changes everything once it is recognized and embraced.

Let's just say for now that a paradigm is a picture of reality that profoundly influences what people *view* as true, possible, and desirable—and what they then *do* to reinforce what they see. It's a whole way of believing and living as if a particular set of understandings and dynamics were the only true/valid/possible/good one available. Please stop for a moment and really let this sink in:

> It's a whole way of believing and living as if a particular set of understandings and dynamics were the only true/valid/possible/good one available.

That's why most paradigms, whether in people or organizations, create what sociologists call a "closed system"—something that is self-defining, self-contained, and self-reinforcing. In individuals this is often called a "fixed mind-set" or being "closed-minded." Anything that doesn't fit or match the closed system's configuration of what is held to be true/valid/possible/good is filtered out and dismissed. Hence, people only see one given set of things as being either possible or desirable, or both.

Barker's most notable phrase in this compelling video is a profoundly disturbing piece of insight that helps to explain why so many people (unnecessarily) fear and resist change. And we think this observation is particularly helpful to leaders as they proceed. He says:

"When a paradigm shifts, everyone goes back to zero!"

In other words, when either your personal view of reality dramatically changes, or the accepted way of viewing and doing things in your society/ culture/organization/profession dramatically changes, what was formerly viewed as true, possible, and desirable loses its tight hold on people, and they find themselves compelled to rethink everything and even start over. No surprise here, but going back to zero, starting over, and rethinking everything are not favorite human pastimes . . . especially for those who benefited significantly from the way the previous paradigm was construed. But we managed to do it, and so can you! And here are some of the insights that helped us manage it.

Education in a Box

Let's be clear. You can't put learning in a box. Nor can you put human capacity, talent, spirit, initiative, creativity, imagination, and character there either. They're the exciting, inspiring, and vital things about being human that we deeply honor and believe that education should do its very best to elevate. Unfortunately, they too often get ignored, suppressed, or undermined in the way education is structured and gets carried out. And that's a key reason why we believe that policies and practices that, either deliberately or inadvertently, downplay or disregard these unique human qualities need to be transcended and removed.

We didn't hold this view nearly as strongly when we began our collaborative work over twenty years ago, but the longer we stayed on the path of deep educational change, the more apparent it became. And one of the reasons behind this realization was our recognition that education had become its own closed system with its own definitions of reality, of what was true/valid/possible/good; its own concepts and vocabulary; its own unique ends and processes; and its own ways of doing business. Translated, that means: Education is its own unique paradigm!

This realization caused in us what is commonly called a "paradigm shift"; and we both went back to zero in looking at it from the outside rather than living within it, as we had been doing. And what leapt out at us once this shift occurred was how boxed-in everything was—something we actually came to call "education in a box."

We came to this viewpoint from two different directions. First, and perhaps most obvious, was that most schools were physically constructed like boxes, with boxes within those boxes. Second, boxes are the antithesis of creativity, freedom, spontaneity, and spirit—the driving elements in Empowermentland. Boxes place boundaries/walls/barriers/structures around things, and those boundaries shape and limit what people can do within them. In fact, they directly foster and embody organizational control over their members through, for example, time schedules, curriculum structures, opportunity patterns, and learning requirements. And while they directly contribute to a sense of regularity and order, boundaries also seriously limit and constrain what can legitimately occur where and when. These constraints, in turn, directly contribute to discouragement and failure in education, which, from an empowerment perspective, concerns us more than anything.

Boxes within Boxes

It's easy to think of the school building and its various rooms as boxes, but we discovered that many of its operating features were defined that way, too. The school box contains lots of other smaller boxes of various kinds, and each of them also has its own unique character, places definite limits and boundaries around what occurs there, and interacts with and reinforces lots of the other boxes as well. Both people and things are defined and hemmed in by these smaller boxes, and everyone is compelled to operate within their combined constraints.

This convergence of structural and operational boxes is, in fact, what we believe leads to the "Specific students of a specific age must learn specific things . . ." syndrome highlighted at the beginning of the chapter. Moreover, as we've been saying to audiences for over a decade:

> These boxes limit, impede, block, constrain, and undermine insightful research, new thinking, emerging possibilities, motivation to change, learning and growth, and real professionalism.

And now that we have your attention on this matter, please consider one more thing that Spady explains more fully in his book *Beyond Counterfeit Reforms*:

> These boxes have been "institutionalized" by educators, "legalized" by policy makers, "internalized" by parents and the public, "legitimated" by the media, and "reinforced" by reform initiatives for so long that many people defend them as if God had invented them.

Translated, this means that our society/culture has come to view the education box and all its smaller boxes both as "givens"—they're just there, period, no questions asked—and as "sacred and inviolable"—"So don't you dare mess with our boxes or [someone] will punish you 'real good.'"

Well, you might need a little recovery time here to reread and reflect on the last page or so of paradigm-shifting perspectives, especially in light of what we said at the very beginning of the chapter about Empowermentland's "Anyone can learn anything at anytime from anywhere . . ." essence.

But when you're ready, we want to share with you more concretely below what we've only described so far in the abstract. On the left is education in a box, with its constellation of fifteen smaller boxes that, we have come to believe, are fundamentally unresponsive to the diverse needs, interests, potentials, learning rates, and maturity levels of individual learners. Next to each box, however, is a significant empowerment age alternative: your future-focused vision and way forward. The contrasts, you will note, are enormous.

The essence of this book is about how you can move your people, your organization, and your community *from* education in a box as their given/absolute/governing paradigm of learning *to* embracing, pursuing, and ultimately implementing these deeper empowerment realities. In different words, your charge as a leader in education is to transform education in a box into what we call an empowering learning community (ELC). Hence, we encourage you to study each comparison carefully, grasp the constraining nature of what's on the left, and begin charting a way to loosen its grip on the way things operate in your organization.

From education in a box	To empowerment paradigm
❐ The Curriculum Subjects B☐X	The world's ever-expanding knowledge base
❐ The Requirements B☐X	The infinite, valuable array of things to explore
❐ The Time/Schedule B☐X	Today's unlimited 24/7/365 access to information
❐ The Grade Level B☐X	Vast differences in learning rates and experiences
❐ The IQ B☐X	Humans' rich array of gifts and talents
❐ The Grading/Marking B☐X	Authentic performance criteria
❐ The Achievement B☐X	The vast array of human abilities and accomplishments
❐ The Standards B☐X	The richness and complexity of life performance
❐ The Test Score B☐X	The complex abilities required in today's work world
❐ The Ranking B☐X	But 50 percent of all people are forced into the "bottom half"
❐ The Access/Eligibility B☐X	Unlimited access to learning via technology
❐ The Opportunity B☐X	Our "anyone can learn anything at anytime" world
❐ The Program/Tracking B☐X	Ever-maturing personal capacities/abilities
❐ The Classroom B☐X	An unlimited array of online and experiential options
❐ The Role/Control B☐X	Self-direction as an invaluable personal attribute

Further Boxed In by Today's Reforms

However, we'll be the first to acknowledge that your job today is way harder than it would have been back in the late nineties when we published the original *Total Leaders* book. Why? What's the difference? The iron grip of the standards-based "reform" movement—that's what! It has not only overwhelmed the educational world in the past decade, it has powerfully strengthened and reinforced every one of the fifteen boxes you've just examined. Yes, every one of them! And in the process it's made many of them smaller, narrower, and more rigid than they already were—which was already way too small, inflexible, and narrow to begin with.

> **In a Nutshell:**
>
> The gap between what now exists in education and what should exist in today's age of empowerment *is far greater than it was just a decade ago.*

Forgive us if this sounds repetitive, but in recent years the world outside of education has evolved from the information age to the age of empowerment, while the world of education has retreated even farther back into its limited and limiting late-nineteenth-century assembly-line paradigm. That paradigm, while well-intentioned back then, emphasizes regularity, standardization, order, and efficiency—none of which characterizes groups of children. The latter vary along a host of important dimensions, which educators face and try to address every day.

But the standards movement and its testing and accountability mandates overlook that profound reality as they put educators under enormous pressure to play by the system's deeply entrenched rules and precedents—embodied in the fifteen boxes. So, in the name of "reform," education has become even more entrenched in its industrial age past, where "specific students of a specific age must learn specific things . . ." and so on. (And if you'd like to gain even more perspective on this, we recommend chapter 6 of Spady's book *Beyond Counterfeit Reforms* and his 2007 paper "The Paradigm Trap.")

The Biggest Box of All

What accounts for this closed-system, self-reinforcing syndrome of structures, orientations, and practices? It's something that Spady calls "educentrism" (again, see *Beyond Counterfeit Reforms* for an extensive explanation of this concept), and it's the biggest box of all! In short, educentrism is the specific and unique way the "modern" education systems of the world are defined, structured, and function. It is, as we noted above, literally a closed, self-reinforcing system unto itself consisting of the fifteen boxes and more. And we educators have all been there, most of us for decades. We were there as young children, then as adolescents, then as late adolescents, and then as young adults. That's when we got formally "trained and certified" to go back there as mature adults and work there as professionals.

The result of all this experience is powerfully captured in something one of our consulting colleagues regularly mentioned to the large audiences of teachers she worked with:

Most of you have been in school since you were five, and school has become your way of life!

And, we would add to her observation: "If school has become your way of life, and it governs how you've learned to think, how you've learned to converse, and how and when you've learned to do what you do, then educentrism is probably your operating paradigm."

But don't despair over this. It was largely ours as well when we began our collaborative work, but we eventually got past it as we looked deeper and deeper into what it meant to prepare young people for a future that was changing before our very eyes. The more we looked at life itself, and the future, and learners as human beings, and the multidimensional nature of learning—all of which we'll be doing with you in some detail in chapter 3—countless educentric things we'd always taken for granted eventually melted away.

It took a long time, and a lot of discipline, and a lot of courage, but eventually we just broke free of all the boxes. And once we did, we knew we couldn't go back—and neither will you! Our paradigm shifted from educentrism to empowerment, and once it did our work took on a special meaning, as will yours. And that's why we're devoting the rest of this book to sharing with you many of the key frameworks and processes that have enabled us to view education from the solid "transformational" starting point and knowledge base it deserves. In so doing, we'll be walking the path together with you that leads to empowering learning communities (ELC).

Going Back to Zero . . . Sort Of

The remainder of this chapter is intended to give you a genuinely transformational perspective on establishing an empowering learning community from the ground up. Yes, we know you're already leading some kind of educational entity, so "zero" isn't exactly where you're starting. Nonetheless, we want to share three key insights with you that will help you and your people get as close to zero as possible in this process.

Note that we learned long ago that "walking your talk" is critical to leadership success. But in the case of education "talking your (intended) walk" may be even more important, simply because education in a box is absolutely loaded with educentric concepts and terminology. And as soon as educentric words are used, people just jump right back into the mind-set of the fifteen boxes—which immediately puts the brakes on transformational thinking.

That's why the language we'll be using throughout this book is as non-educentric as it can be—because that's the paradigm perspective we're inviting you to take here. And that's why your "thought, talk, and walk" all have to be as transformational as possible. After all, as we describe in chapter 6 of *Total Leaders 2.0*, you're going to be both the lead learner and the lead teacher for your people in this inspiring journey to becoming an ELC.

If you want to create a genuine empowering learning community, then . . .

1. Avoid using educentric thinking and terminology at all costs!
2. Never ask an educentric question if you want a non-educentric answer!
3. And . . . *never* accept an educentric answer to a non-educentric question!

To assist you in this very early stage of the journey, we're going to share another "from–to" framework with you. We've developed, shared, and collected mountains of useful ones over the years, very similar to the education in a box one earlier. They serve as concrete reminders of the alternative, non-educentric ways we can view, describe, and do education, and we are encouraging you to continually recharge your non-educentric batteries by going back and rereading any of the ones you find in this

From a Limiting Reformer Orientation/Educentric Paradigm	To an Expansive Transformer Orientation/Empowerment Paradigm
In-the-box viewpoint	Outside-the-box viewpoint
Content-focused learning	Inner-focused learning
Disciplinary curriculum	Trans-disciplinary curriculum
Rational/logical thinking	Divergent/lateral thinking
Teacher-initiated/classroom-based learning	Learner-initiated/life experience learning
Graded structure and learning opportunities	Nongraded structure and learning opportunities
Academic achievement and advancement	Personal development and maturity
Transmission of accepted knowledge and understandings	Exploration of unique insights and possibilities
External expectations, control, and rewards	Internal motivation, control, and fulfillment
Premium on IQ learning	Focus on EQ development
Competitive organizational ethic	Collaborative organizational ethic
Quantitative measures of success	Qualitative measures of development
Closed-system thinking and operations	Open-system thinking and operations
Scheduled learning opportunities	Flexible learning opportunities
Getting right answers	Asking deeper questions
Adults as control and evaluation agents	Adults as learning and performance role models

book. So here's one you might want to use again and again as your change effort proceeds. It's one of our most recent, and it contains a number of very important paradigm shifts.

Yes, we believe this one is worth a lot of reflection time, and, in fact, you might consider using many of the "to" elements as key features of the ELC that you ultimately decide to create.

Defining Your Empowering Learning Community

At the end of chapter 6 in *Total Leaders 2.0*, we officially made the link to what is the heart of this book—what we've been calling an empowering learning community (ELC). That discussion was about what educators could do to create a detailed "vision" for the kind of learning community they wanted to create and be a part of. Then earlier in this chapter we defined an organizational vision as:

> a clear, detailed picture of what your organization will be doing when operating at its ideal best to accomplish its purpose. This ideal describes the very best job you could possibly do based on your highest aspirations and deepest motivations. It's your roadmap to success. Without it your people won't have a clear picture of the change you seek to make.

With that as a reminder, let's proceed under the assumption that the remainder of this book, chapters 2 through 7, represents our vision of an ideal ELC—an inspiring picture that makes your journey out of educentrism more than worth it. This certainly will make it one of the most detailed and elaborate visions ever created, but that's because a lot of explanation will go along with the descriptive elements in each chapter. And let's add another assumption: There isn't just one way of defining, or implementing, an ELC. There are many potential templates. But the one we're choosing is truly systemic, future focused, learner centered, deeply empowering, and non-educentric (which may be the redundant criterion if you truly embrace and implement the other four). And if you hope to live up to the term "transformational," we certainly wouldn't want you to overlook or omit any of these five.

The Five Essential Components

So as long as we're offering assumptions about defining an ELC, here's a five-part one:

1. Every educational organization has a philosophy and ratio-nale—a fundamental reason for its existence including its beliefs, paradigm thinking, knowledge base, core values and principles, and purpose. So does an ELC.

2. Every educational organization has a culture—"the way we do things around here . . . when no one is looking!"—both visible and subtle norms, symbols, and pressures to think and behave in ways that earn you the approval of others. So does an ELC.

3. Every educational organization has intended outcomes for its learners—what it aspires for its learners to know, do, and be as the result of the experiences that define both their and the organization's success. So does an ELC.

4. Every educational organization has a learning system—the array of learning opportunities, experiences, and processes that enable learners to accomplish the organization's intended outcomes. So does an ELC.

5. Every educational organization has a support structure—a constellation of physical and technological resources, adminis-trative procedures, and personnel mechanisms that enable its learning system to function effectively. So does an ELC.

These five systemic assumptions enable us to look at educational organizations in a rather concise and powerful way. They all have philoso-phies, cultures, outcomes, learning systems, and support structures—their operating components. These are the system's essential "nouns." Take one away and the system loses direction, goes out of whack, or both.

Now all you have to do to get a sense of how educational organiza-tions vary from each other is add some adjectives to the nouns. No, we're not being clever; there's enormous power in the adjectives because they add the qualitative flavoring to what are otherwise pretty neutral operating components. So let's try one. Just go back and put the word "educentric" in front of each of the five as you read its statement, and see what you get. Correct: education in a box! (Pass the aspirin, please!) Now if you want to brighten your day a bit, go back and put the word "empowering" there instead. Feel better? Whew, so do we!

Now what we're suggesting here is clearly not quite as simple as re-labeling things, but you immediately could see and feel the difference as you inserted the two different defining qualities to these generic system components. In our case, in fact, it has taken many years to find the adjectives that really represent the "transformational" essence of every-thing expressed in the two "from–to" frameworks we've examined in this chapter. So here they are in a diagram that reflects a number of important theoretical factors that we don't need to get into at the moment. Just absorb it and get a sense of how different it is from the fifteen boxes that constitute educentric schools.

Figure 1.1 contains three critical things that we'd like you to take forward as you consider each component in detail. First, each component is defined/shaped by at least one powerful adjective that defines its fun-

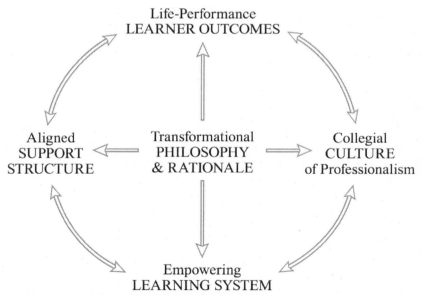

Figure 1.1. The key components of an empowering learning community.

damental character. Second, everything emanates out of and is shaped by the ELC's transformational philosophy and rationale. It is truly purpose, values, and vision driven, and we'll describe it in detail in chapter 3. Third, each of the other operational components are interconnected in a pattern of mutual influence, including the components on the vertical and horizontal axes. Everything influences and supports everything else.

The Five Wellsprings

But there are more adjectives/qualities to add to the mix that actually represent the essence of an ELC in less technical language. We call them the "wellsprings" of harmonious—and we might add, empowered—living, learning, and leadership; and they're introduced and fully integrated into the *Total Leaders 2.0* framework from chapter 4 on.

As it happens, the five wellsprings all start with the letter "C." Hence, many of our colleagues know and work with them as "the five Cs." But these five "C" words happen to be quite versatile. They can be expressed in noun, adjective, or adverb form and, therefore, can directly support the model in various ways. Moreover, we've learned that as adjectives and adverbs, they can apply to an entire range of social entities . . . from individuals to teams to organizations to cultures to societies and even to civilizations.

So here they are, expressed as nouns that ground the concepts themselves. These definitions and the other examples below were developed several years ago by members of the HeartLight Learning Community, an alternative high school in Port Elizabeth, South Africa.

- **Consciousness**. Our deep and full awareness of who we are and how we can respond to life in each moment.

- **Creativity**. Our intense curiosity to explore and express our rich imaginations and life's boundless possibilities.

- **Collaboration**. Our active participation with others in endeavors that enhance the standing and well-being of all.

- **Competence**. The willing application of one's knowledge and skills to produce and achieve things of value.

- **Compassion**. Our deep sensitivity to our connection to all living things and our commitment to honor it.

Now with these definitions in mind, consider them in adverb form as they describe both the ELC as an entity and each of its members:

- Functioning consciously, with intention and integrity

- Functioning creatively, with inspiration and imagination

- Functioning collaboratively, with inclusion and involvement

- Functioning competently, with initiative and industry

- Functioning compassionately, with intervention and influence

Or, as a further example, consider them as qualities your ELC would desire in its graduates as they step out the door into Empowermentland:

- As conscious contributors

- As creative contributors

- As collaborative contributors

- As competent contributors

- As compassionate contributors

Our experience with the wellsprings has been uniformly positive, especially among parents and educators who believe that education is about way more than cramming academically approved content into learners on a predetermined schedule. Their focus on the learner, the human being in the learning equation, makes the five Cs very appealing because they resonate with their sense of what makes life really work harmoniously. This has been particularly true in both South Africa and Australia, where we have done extensive consulting work in the past decade, and in our collaborative work with educators from Russia and Georgia in an initiative called Beautiful School International.

And Now for the Details . . .

The remainder of this book provides the "meat" that you can put on the skeleton framework of an ELC just provided. Chapter 2 focuses on establishing a collegial culture of professionalism. We're addressing it first because without a coherent, cohesive, and professional way of functioning, the process of getting the other four components in place will founder. Next we'll address the nerve center of your ELC: its transformational philosophy and rationale. Plan to give this (chapter 3) a lot of time and attention, because it's the bedrock of your organization.

Perhaps the biggest paradigm stretch for your people will come in chapter 4, where we explain the whys, whats, and hows of deriving life performance learner outcomes. We'll be showing exciting examples from across the world that really symbolize learning transformation and empowerment in future-focused form. And on its heels comes the heavy-lifting parts of your change process: implementing an empowering learning system (chapters 5 and 6) and building an aligned support structure (chapter 7). Expect to see what the terms "systemic" and "restructuring" really mean from a paradigm change perspective, and what the essence of a true "learning community" is—in action!

So keep reading. It's the visionary journey you hoped you could take when you decided to become an educator!

CHAPTER TWO
ESTABLISHING A COLLEGIAL CULTURE OF PROFESSIONALISM

Culture is the sum total of all the shared, taken-for-granted assumptions that a group has learned throughout its history. It is the residue of success.

—Edgar Schein

That's just the way we do things around here.

—waitress at Bayou Bob's Restaurant in Denver

Here you see two parallel diagrams. You just saw figure 2.1 near the end of chapter 1. It portrays the five grounding components of an empowering learning community (ELC), and it serves as the framework on which you can build the vision of the ideal educational system you and your colleagues and constituents seek to implement. We have highlighted the component that we'll be addressing in this chapter as your step 1 in creating that vision—your collegial culture of professionalism.

Below figure 2.1 is a parallel diagram showing the five corresponding components of our Total Leaders model. This defining diagram originally appears near the end of chapter 4 in *Total Leaders 2.0*. Here too we've highlighted the leadership domain that most directly impacts on creating and sustaining the organizational culture you desire. We call it relational leadership, and we encourage you to study it in more detail in chapter 5 of that book; there we focus on the in-depth change process in which Total Leaders engage. It's called strategic design, and it explains how leaders establish the five critical pillars of change described early in chapter 1.

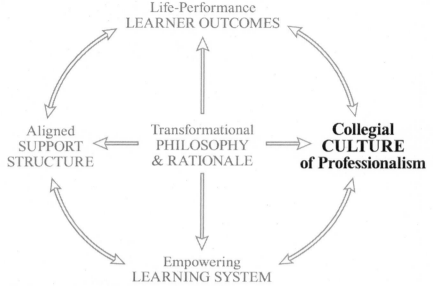

Life-Performance
LEARNER OUTCOMES

Aligned
SUPPORT
STRUCTURE

Transformational
PHILOSOPHY
& RATIONALE

**Collegial
CULTURE
of Professionalism**

Empowering
LEARNING SYSTEM

Figure 2.1.   Focusing on an ELC's organizational culture.

VISIONARY
Creative & Cutting Edge
Vision

SERVICE
Compassionate
& Dedicated
Support

AUTHENTIC
Conscious
& Ethical
Purpose

RELATIONAL
Collaborative
& Collegial
Ownership

QUALITY
Competent & Expert
Capacity

Figure 2.2.   The parallel emphasis of Total Leadership 2.0.

Our argument in *TL2.0* is that organizations need to have in place an effective way of functioning culturally and interpersonally if they hope to succeed in implementing any of the steps/processes that strategic design entails, and that's what relational leadership is all about. Stated simply, if your people are constantly at odds, consistently pulling in different directions, not talking to each other, and sabotaging every good idea that's ever proposed, then you're not only in the deepest of doo-doo, you haven't a prayer of getting out of all the educentric boxes described in chapter 1 of this book.

That's why we're beginning our more detailed description of an ELC's vision by addressing the kind of culture it's going to have. And from what you can see in the top diagram, two key words prevail: *collegial* and *professionalism*!

Cultures, Cultures Everywhere . . .

Cultures are soft but powerful forces that control the thoughts and actions of people within organizations of all kinds, be they families, businesses, or maybe even ELCs. We're sure you've heard of strong yet caring people described as "using a velvet hammer" to make things happen. Well, as much as we obviously dislike controlling boxes, we must agree that a collegial culture of professionalism does, in effect, create a box . . . a soft, velvet, and powerful box that is totally supportive of collegiality, professionalism, and everyone learning in community with each other.

The reality is that no organization gets to choose if they will or will not have a culture. They *will* have one! The only choices leaders have in the matter is to decide if they want to be consciously aware of the culture and proactive in determining what qualities it will have.

Most organizational cultures are not planned—in fact, they're not even thought about until there are problems with "attitude," "lack of cooperation," "sloppy work," or some other negative behavior that has become an organizational norm that is causing things to unravel. Culture is the silent, unrecognized source of problems that show themselves throughout organizations. Much like hypertension, which is said to be the silent killer because people don't feel it and aren't aware of it, negative cultures are the silent killer of positive attitudes, creativity and initiative, productivity, and ultimately, the organization itself (think General Motors).

Therefore, nothing as important and powerful as organizational culture should be left to chance. Which is why TL2.0s are conscious and intentional about creating a culture that is based on the assumptions, beliefs, values, and norms consistent with empowerment, consistent with collegiality, consistent with professionalism, and consistent with the effective operation of an authentic learning community.

Organizational cultures can be . . .	
Strong	Weak
Aligned	Discordant
Helpful	Harmful
Clear	Fuzzy
Overt	Covert
Functional	Dysfunctional
Deliberate	Spontaneous
Flexible	Bureaucratic

but there *will* be culture!

The Power of Established Cultures

Established cultures in established organizations are difficult to change. As Schein's definition above suggests, cultures are created by how we've been successful and how we've coped with the demands of the job as we see them. Effective relational leaders don't wait for problems to surface before focusing on culture. Hence, the time to establish the positive culture you want is in the beginning, as you create a new organization, the day you take your new leadership position—or *now*, "the first day of the rest of your life."

Although established cultures are slow and difficult to change, they can be changed and frequently they *must* be changed if the organization is to survive and grow. Let's do the math. A new leader should always find that at least one-third of his inherited staff agree with him, support him, and want him to be successful. National norms regarding personnel turnover is about 12 percent per year, so after three years the new leader has probably hired another one-third of his staff. Assuming that new staff selections were based upon empowerment attitudes and talents, the TL2.0 now has about two-thirds of his staff on his side—a solid majority, even if he didn't "get the wrong people off of the bus." Just as a new president at some time must stop blaming his predecessor for his organization's problems, so must the TL2.0 take ownership for his organization's culture after two or three years.

Nearly all leadership gurus speak to culture, and most of our excellent leadership reads tell of the power that culture has over what people say and don't say, and what they do and don't do. Culture is so pervasive that we usually don't even realize that we're editing what we say and do for fear of recrimination. It is good for the TL2.0 to know that the most effective organizations of the day work to create a culture that values, honors, and rewards openness, cooperation, future focusing, innovation, quality, success, and continuous improvement. Leaders can't go wrong by shooting for these cultural targets.

A number of years ago Terrence Deal, an educator at heart, and Allan Kennedy wrote *Corporate Cultures*, and in it they made the fuzzy concept of culture come alive. The book has been updated with a new title, *The New Corporate Cultures*, and it remains one of the better resources for understanding the subtle nature and the awesome power of culture. In fact, they make the special point that culture is more easily understood when viewed through its tangible forms. That's why you'll learn much about the values and the culture of a school system by taking a tour, looking at what's on the walls, seeing what the hallway trophy case tells you, studying the (outdated) strategic plan, listening to the stories that are told by the "brown baggers" in the office lounge, studying the school calendar to learn what the system celebrates.

Another clear path to determining the real culture of an organization is to listen closely to learn who the heroes and heroines of the system are. Are they those who are champions of learners, or those in the lounge who belittle students? Are they those who are excited about an experiment they are trying in their classroom, or those who are giving a quick look at the yellow-edged notes they will use in their 1:00 class? Are they those who use transformational technology to personalize learning, or those who think that technology is ruining our kids?

Perceptive and proactive leaders of the culture identify the system's tangible forms of culture and begin to change them to be consistent with the values and vision of their new LC. The trophy case formerly dominated by boys' athletics is then balanced by a display of successful school graduates who have chosen community service roles. Heroes and heroines whose

> **Tangible Forms of Culture**
>
> - Heroes/heroines
> - Rituals
> - Ceremonies
> - Traditions
> - Symbols
> - Shared values
> - Stories
>
> —Terrence Deal

attitudes and actions are contrary to the LC vision are subtly replaced over time by those who model the principles of professionalism identified in the LC's strategic design. But never fear—it's still OK for you to have that "hole-in-one plaque" prominently displayed on your office wall . . . although maybe it should be under rather than above the listing of "Our Strongest Beliefs about Children and Learning."

The Leader as Culture Shaper

Establishing a collegial culture of professionalism begins with the leader, and begins on the first day the leader begins his or her new job as the leader of an educentric "school system" that is destined to become a vibrant ELC. Establishing a culture begins when the leader chooses not to park in the space labeled, "This space reserved for the school superintendent. All others will be towed." So he or she parks in the first unmarked space available. Culture creation continues when the leader walks through the door and already knows the name of the receptionist; when she introduces herself as Brenda Hansen, not as Dr. Hansen; when he or she meets her secretary and refers to the secretary as his or her new teammate; and when the leader immediately moves the desk from the middle to against a wall and asks the custodian to find a small round table with four chairs where he or she can work with people who come to the office.

We could go on throughout the leader's total first day on the job, but we expect you've gotten the message. The organization's informal network will quickly spread the word of Dr. Hansen's entrance throughout the system, and a "collegial culture of professionalism" will have begun.

Now you might question Dr. Hansen's desire to be on a first-name basis with her staff. Does that create a sense of "professionalism" or the lack thereof? Allow that Brenda may well be thinking: "Collegiality sounds a lot like egalitarianism . . . I don't want to put myself above anyone by attaching 'Dr.' to my name, having a private parking space, or having the only key to the executive bathroom . . . I want to demonstrate that I value collegiality, and I want to model that value." Sometimes modeling is just natural, and sometimes it's intentional. No matter which one, the leader should know that people are watching, interpreting, and judging his or her every move.

Please allow a personal story about Chuck here that is relevant for two reasons: (1) impactful modeling is not always planned, and (2) stories are powerful carriers of culture.

It was my first year as a superintendent in Colorado and I was facing about four hundred staff members at the all-school orientation that kicked off the school year. My topic was something like "An Inspirational Vision for Our District." I was nervous. It was August and hot, the overhead projector added to the warmth, and so about three or four minutes into my presentation I took off my sport coat and tossed it over a chair. There was a loud and unified gasp from the crowd. I immediately checked to see if my fly was open. It wasn't. (Thank you, Almighty One!)

Now if I had been more secure in front of our entire staff that day, I might have stopped and said, "What was that all about?" But I wasn't that secure—so I continued with my presentation as though nothing had happened.

At the end of my talk, I thought that it had all gone quite well, and I was rather pleased with myself. Later, I asked my colleagues about what had caused the unified gasp. They chuckled as they told me about my predecessor. He was a young, short, authoritarian leader who had established system-wide rules for male leaders . . . and they were *all* male. One could only remove his suit coat if he were in his office, if he were alone, and if the office door was closed. And in front of all four hundred, I had casually removed my coat and broken all three rules in one decisive gesture.

One month later, I doubt that anyone remembered what I had said that day—but nearly all of them remembered that I had taken off my coat. For most, taking off my coat was a clear signal that things were going to change. For some, it pointed toward less rigidity, to more open-ness . . . gee, maybe even to a collegial culture of professionalism.

So, back to Chuck's two points for the story. Stories are powerful vehicles for describing culture. The leadership literature of late indicates that effec-tive leaders are good storytellers. The leadership team laughed about this incident for Chuck's entire eight years in that system, and the story grew to include positive attributes that had not even happened. Second point: "Who you are is how you lead." People are watching. You are on stage even when you are not on stage. Relational leaders do most of their modeling without being intentional about it. It's just who they are (for good or for bad).

What Collegiality Looks and Feels Like

Learning communities, as we describe them here, may be a new concept to almost everyone. Since there are few places to go to see them in ac-tion—save some Montessori and Waldorf schools—many may view them as bold and somewhat scary experiments. They may believe deeply in the vision presented here, but there is no formula they can follow for imple-mentation. Much like NASA when President Kennedy made his "man on the moon" announcement, they don't know everything they need to know to make it happen. They will prepare as best they can; but out of necessity, much of their learning will take place as things unfold. They will learn as they go, and from the ideas of other recent implementers. But here's the kicker about collegiality that they must keep in mind:

> **No one of us is as smart as all of us. Given this bold undertak-ing, we need each other's ideas, support, feedback, and wisdom more than ever.**

To bolster this thought, here are some familiar words/examples that help illustrate what powerful collegial relationships are like:

- **Teams/Team Members**. Athletic teams easily come to mind. Much like the Lakers need both guards and centers, both offense and defense, both feeders and shooters, collegial teams are strengthened by a diversity of talents. If we all have the same experiences and we all think the same, collegial teams won't be that much stronger than their best and brightest member.

- **Equals/Egalitarianism**. Just because we are different from each other doesn't mean that we don't have both critical and important knowledge and talents to contribute. Just because I am an assistant principal doesn't mean that the superintendent can't learn from me. Collegiality is basically oblivious to hierarchy, but resonates with talent.

- **Work Groups**. More and more, it's work groups and not individuals that solve problems and create new, innovative products and services. Work groups are frequently brought together to work on a specific project based on their background, their expertise, and their interest/passion.

Collegiality is about openly and rather unconditionally sharing— sharing information, expertise, talents, responsibility, and rewards. Collegial groups don't horde information, contacts, or resources. Through all of this interaction, all of this sharing, all of this problem solving, we learn and we grow as professionals. Continuous and meaningful learning may well be the top personal reward for being a colleague to others. And collegiality also requires highly developed interpersonal communication skills, relationship-building skills, group process skills, problem-solving skills, and conflict management skills. Here's the short list of each:

- **Interpersonal Communication Skills**. The ability to paraphrase, to describe behavior, to describe feelings, to check for the perceptions of others, to provide constructive feedback, to receive candid feedback.

- **Relationship-Building Skills**. Being authentic, listening, empathy, being "other-conscious," trustworthiness, being supportive.

- **Group Process Skills**. Creating an agenda, listening, questioning, providing information, clarifying, summarizing, checking for consensus.

- **Problem-Solving Skills**. Problem classification and clarification, applying data, applying theory and research, brainstorming solutions, forcefield analysis, testing potential solutions for their effectiveness, ensuring follow-through.

- **Conflict Management Skills**. Candor, thinking and applying "win-win," protecting everyone's dignity, clearly stating and clarifying potential compromises, summarizing and clarifying decisions.

Notice how many of these skills reflect Daniel Goleman's writings—a great resource for understanding our relationships and ourselves. We have studied all five of his books, recommend them all, and suggest two that are particularly germane to this issue: *Emotional Intelligence* and *Social Intelligence*. Stephen Covey's perennial best-seller, *The Seven Habits of Highly Effective People*, also remains very high on our list of valuable resources. Three of these habits focus directly on relationship-building skills: (1) Seek first to understand and then to be understood, (2) Think win-win, and (3) Create synergy. Those three habits pretty well describe collegiality. In addition, Susan Scott's bestseller *Fierce Conversations* is excellent as a tool for readying oneself for those tough conversations that we dread but know are necessary.

Given all of this input, it might be wise for you to take a break here and consider whom you'd put on your collegial all-star team to design and implement your ELC. This group would come together as colleagues, as equals, and as team members to work toward the realization of your bold ELC vision. Who are they, and would they really be constructive contributors? Given the nature and diversity of your challenge, here's a team we'd strongly recommend—and please forgive us for nominating ourselves:

- **Bill Spady**, to provide insights, expertise, and vision regarding philosophy, mission, purpose, and your ultimate learner outcomes/results.

- **Steve Jobs**, to provide insights on how we could use transformational technology to personalize learning for everyone.

- **Chuck Schwahn**, to help us visualize an instructional delivery system capable of creating a personalized, empowering daily learning schedule for each learner.

- **Bob Marzano**, to help us focus on the research (what we know) regarding learners, learning, and teaching.

- **Bea McGarvey**, to help us know how best to create positive learning climates and facilitate learning for individuals and groups.

- **Kathy Countryman**, to use her TL2.0 skills to lead and manage our ELC with passion, courage, and class.

- **Bill Gates**. Just thought that it would be "ni$e" to have Bill around, but he'll probably insist on being team captain.

Lest we forget, should you be able to pick your colleagues, collegiality is a lot more fun if you really like your colleagues, laugh a lot with them, and would select them to join your group, especially if the event were a fishing trip to eastern Siberia.

From Bureaucrat to Professional

Unfortunately, it is difficult to refer to today's education establishment as a "profession." We strongly implied it in chapter 1 but didn't state it overtly. Our typical educentric school systems and the "reforms" they're forced to implement just don't foster or fit the definition or criteria of a "total professional" that we described in chapter 4 of *TL2.0* and embraced in our 2.0 model shown above in figure 2.2:

Ethical, cutting-edge, collegial, expert, and dedicated.

Especially the "cutting-edge" part. This is no fault of the educators themselves or a reflection of who they are as individuals. It's the product of the bureaucratic system in which they must function if they are to be employed, and it's why we're so committed to the notion of creating ELCs in place of educentric "schools in a box."

CHAPTER TWO

The Power of the Bureaucratic Paradigm

Yes, after over four decades of each of us being heavily involved in educational change and improvement, we've finally surrendered to the often-heard criticism that today's public schools (with their fifteen boxes) are bureaucratic monopolies, and that education is an industry, not a profession. Please understand: The above assertion is not a blanket condemnation of individual educators, nor is it their "fault." Every educator has a choice about how they view and do their work, and these paradigms vary enormously. In fact, you probably know people for whom each of these viewpoints holds:

- "Education's my job, and I show up every day as required."
- "I'm putting in my time till retirement, and it's only three years away."
- "I'm a loyal and dedicated employee, and I consistently do what's required."
- "I'm an up-to-date expert on what I teach, and that matters most to me."
- "I'm continuously upgrading my ability to meet each learner's unique needs."

And there are clearly other prominent "role identities" we might have included in this list.

The larger issue here is that educators have official roles to play, and those roles are prescribed in the regulations and rules that define the system itself. Unfortunately, the dynamics of those regulatory constraints foster one of the most detrimental influences to real professionalism in education: administrative convenience!

As Bill has been pointing out to audiences for over thirty years, it's way easier to let the clock, schedule, and calendar run things, than it is to meet the challenge of responding in a timely way to the learning needs, levels, interests, and accomplishments of individual learners. However, that's when "real professionalism" in education emerges—though we'll be the first to admit that it's not easy to execute (yet chapters 5 and 6 will explain how it's *way* easier today that it was even a decade ago).

Why is it so easy to surrender to these time-defined, bureaucratic mechanisms? Because neither educators nor the public is willing to acknowledge the elephant in the room that's really determining how everything else happens. It's education's hidden mission: crowd control! Because hundreds, if not thousands, of children are literally crowded into confined spaces under the supervision of relatively few adults, there has to be a way of organizing and managing this formidable challenge. Under these circumstances, it's simply a lot easier to let uniform, routine, standardized, bureaucratic mechanisms like the clock, schedule, and calendar take over, than to manage this mass of humanity in more flexible, discretionary, and empowering ways . . . which brings us right back to administrative convenience.

Individual teachers do their best to handle this challenge behind the closed doors of their classrooms, but the larger organizational context sets the tone and expectation for all of them. In other words, the need to bureaucratically manage the clients/people in the system helps create and foster a bureaucratic culture rather than a professional one.

However, we don't believe that education's "bureaucracy" problem results from its unwillingness to admit to there being one and committing to do something about it. We sincerely believe that the problem is a layer deeper than that:

> We don't even know that we're bureaucratic because most educators have literally been in school—the fifteen boxes—their entire lives. "School" has become their paradigm—their educational reality.

As a result, they think that "having school" is just that: It's "having school"—and "school" means being in the educentric boxes. "Haven't we always done it that way before? And how could it be 'school' without the boxes? They're actually the defining elements in what 'school' is." In addition, most educators haven't taken the time to see how closely the structures, policies, and procedures of school systems resemble those of the bureaucracies that many people love to hate: the postal service, the DMV, General Motors, and the Catholic Church. (Chuck's a Catholic, so he thinks we have political and spiritual "cover" for saying that.)

So, let's conclude this particular discussion with two propositions. First, schools operate like, are structured like, and function like typical bureaucracies. Hence, we think it's fair to label most public schools "bureaucracies." (If it looks like a duck, walks like a duck, quacks like a duck . . . yes, it's probably a duck.) Second, if you're the administrator of a school or school district that functions like a bureaucracy, it's fair to call you a "bureaucrat." (We barely whispered that, and . . . "What happens in Vegas, stays . . .")

This is tough for us to say, but until educators acknowledge their educentric/bureaucratic orientation and the grip it has on their organization's culture, the only change they'll experience—based on the levels of change we described in chapter 1—is "cosmetic." Our other label for this is "technical tinkering," and it's what Theodore Sizer meant in 1983 when he wrote about "putting another coat of paint on the Model T" and calling it "change." And if you'll allow us one more candid observation, we'd like to alert you to "the three Rs" that foster and reinforce bureaucratic thinking, action, and cultures: regulations, routines, and rituals. Need we say more about administrative convenience?

The Principles of Professionalism

We have designed a rather popular workshop called "Principles of Professionalism" that is based on a very important framework presented in our original *Total Leaders* book and repeated in *TL2.0*. (In fact, these principles alone would be a powerful shaper of an ELC's culture, and we recommend that you view and use them that way.) One of the activities we use in the workshop involves having participants (usually all from the same organization) define what "professional" means to them by answering the question, "How would you know one if you saw one?" Here are the ten principles we show them as prompts:

- **Accountability**. Taking responsibility for the content and the process of decisions made, actions taken, and the resulting outcomes.

- **Improvement**. A commitment to continuously enhance the quality of personal and organizational performance, the processes used to generate results, and the results themselves.

- **Alignment**. The purposeful, direct matching of decisions, resources, and organizational structures with the organization's declared purpose, vision, and core values.

- **Inquiry**. The honest search for personal and organizational purpose, rich and broad perspectives on complex issues, and a deep understanding of ideas and possibilities.

- **Contribution**. Freely giving and investing one's attention, talent, and resources to enhance the quality and success of meaningful endeavors.

- **Clarity**. Embodied in the open, honest, and articulate communication of one's direction and priorities, the information needed for making sound decisions and taking positive action, and the expectations that surround work and personal relationships.

- **Win-Win**. A commitment to achieving and experiencing mutual benefit in the agreements people make, the relationships they establish, and the rewards they obtain from the contributions they make.

- **Future Focusing**. Conducting a thorough and consistent study of the shifts, trends, and future conditions that redefine a profession, industry, or organization, and taking a visionary and far-reaching view of emerging possibilities.

- **Inclusiveness**. Consistent commitment to maximizing both the range of opportunities for success available to organizational members, and the number of people included in relevant and meaningful organizational decisions.

- **Connection**. One's deep and genuine relationship with, and appreciation of, the value, intellectual, and feeling dimensions in oneself and others.

And we also add as prompts the five characteristics of the Total Professional noted above:

Ethical, cutting-edge, collegial, expert, and dedicated.

Invariably, after considering this rich mix of possibilities, the number one criterion on the lists that participants create is that professionals act from a sound and ever-evolving knowledge and research base.

Real professionals seek out and apply what has been proven to be true. This embodies a powerful combination of inquiry, future focusing, cutting-edge, and expert.

Please take a moment to let the four factors in the shaded box sink in. Then ask yourself what kinds of arrangements your organization has formally established to make them the norm for "how we do things around here." Do you have regular study groups about research on learning, brain development, instructional processes, and high-level outcomes? Or brainstorming sessions on how to provide learning opportunities on a more timely, learner-centered basis? If not, start them now. Your ELC can't get off the ground or thrive without them.

And when you do that, be sure to distribute copies of chapter 3 (coming up), because it provides some paradigm-expanding insights about learners, learning, learning systems, and life that will absolutely challenge the myths surrounding educentrism from all angles.

Personal Bias

And let's not overlook another common obstacle to professionalism: personal bias. How many times have you heard students complain that their teacher has a grudge against them, and, therefore, lowered their grade because she didn't like them? Or that an administrator has given a poor evaluation to a teacher because he didn't agree with his personal philosophy or politics? In either case—and there are untold numbers of them out there with slightly different details—you've got a classic case of an educator not behaving professionally; that is, an educator with a clear bias toward the "subordinate" individual, either "playing favorites" or putting someone on their "blacklist" and withholding opportunities or kudos they deserve.

If you consider the principles and other criteria just mentioned, situations like this reveal that you've got a breakdown in accountability on your hands, plus serious shortcomings in the "ethical" department. And nothing damages morale and contaminates a culture faster than allowing violations of professional ethics to start, then continue unchecked and unchallenged—especially when they emanate from the person in a position of leadership. If you haven't done so, please give a good read to chapters 3 and 6 in *TL2.0*—particularly our discussion of a leader's moral foundation and how it's the ultimate deal-maker/deal-breaker in terms of credibility and trust.

Professionalism That Supports ELCs

Moving from a bureaucratic mind-set and bureaucratic procedures to a client-centered mind-set and accompanying behaviors is the most pervasive and powerful of all "professional" attributes. But there are other significant ones too that, when aligned with an inspirational vision, create the synergy required to make an ELC a reality. As we note in chapter 7 of *TL2.0*, alignment, job one of service leaders, is the WD-40 that allows for friction-free energy to be focused on the realization of an ELC's vision. Professional educators who embrace a vision of empowerment

- **Are collegial**. They work closely with others who have similar interests and goals. They are egalitarian in their relationships and openly share their new insights and learnings with others. Professional educators in collegial relationships hold the power to create and sustain an ELC.

- **Are dedicated to practice**. It's not just theory; it's theory into practice, and practice is the right word. They plan theory-based interventions with researching/learning in mind, they learn from their experiences and results, and they share what they learn with their colleagues—colleagues who are doing the same type of sharing with them.

- **Embrace a code of ethics**. Professionals are clear about their moral foundation; they consistently apply their moral code as they work/practice, and they monitor and confront their colleagues when they sense something happening that is not in the best interest of young learners.

- **Are passionate**. They select their profession and their career because of its compelling purpose. Their personal goals and the mission of their chosen profession are closely aligned. Their passion, directed by their code of ethics, leads them to value quality and to create quality products and services. They take pride in what they do, take responsibility for what they have done, and willingly hold themselves accountable for results/ outcomes.

- **Are lifelong learners**. Maybe this attribute needn't even be stated, but continuous learning and development is the natural MO for the professional. We expect our doctors to know the latest regarding health, and we expect our professional educators to know the latest and best about learners and learning, about leading, and maybe even the latest and best about living the good life. This is what "cutting-edge" and "expert" are all about.

- **Are self-aware.** Professionals know who they are, what they value, what they want to accomplish, and their vision of what they want to be in the future. They have done their "inner work" (again see chapter 3 of *TL2.0*). They know their talents . . . and the areas in which they are not so talented; they reflect on their assumptions and beliefs; and they are aware of and monitor their biases.

So, Who's a "Professional" and a Leader?

When we hear or use the term "professional," we tend to think of architects, lawyers, doctors, athletes, and so on. But contrary to the conventional use of the term, we believe that the nameplate on the office door and the diplomas on the wall aren't the determiners of there being a "professional" occupying the room.

Professionalism is determined by mind-sets, values, and behaviors. We've all known those with professional law degrees who are shysters, and we've all known custodians who were true professionals. For us, custodians who talk quality and best-practice techniques with their fellow custodians, who love their work and are dedicated to creating attractive learning environments for children, who embrace self-imposed rules and standards for their work, who experiment with floor cleaners and share their results with their colleagues, and who read and study *Consumer Reports* and other information related to their work *are* professionals in the "authentic" sense of the word.

A professional like this is very much a "lead learner" and "lead teacher" as we've described them in *TL2.0*, so hire them for your ELC! They're making choices in their life that make the world a better place for everyone, and that's one of the deepest expressions of empowerment we can think of. And that certainly ranks miles above the contributions of the educational administrator who thoughtlessly surrenders to administrative convenience and the bureaucratic regulations, routines, and rituals that are inconsistent with what all of us know about students and learning. In fact, one of our favorite overheads states, "Total Leaders Everywhere!" and it's perfect for this hypothetical custodian and every member of an ELC.

In a Nutshell:

It's the role you play, not the position you hold, that makes you a leader and a professional—and positively shapes your organization's culture.

The "who you are is how you lead" premise underlying Total Leadership comes into play big time regarding culture. That's why leaders in all kinds of positions in an organization are responsible for creating, monitoring, and sustaining a collegial culture of professionalism. Their collective appearance, attitude, beliefs, values, and behaviors are major forces that ultimately determine what an ELC honors and embodies. In effect, they are stepping into the domain we call relational leadership, and in that role they're proactive in

- Involving their colleagues in determining the culture they wish to create

- Identifying behaviors consistent and inconsistent with that culture

- Monitoring and coaching for the behaviors their ideal culture requires

- Confronting those whose actions detract from that ideal culture

- Rewarding the actions of those who foster a collegial culture of professionalism

In short, relational leaders know that culture is too important to leave to chance, so they don't.

Eventually, a collegial culture of professionalism *is* created by

- What you model
- What you honor
- What you accept
- What you reward

The Five Wellsprings of Harmonious Functioning

Finally, we would not do justice to the issue of organizational culture if we omitted the five wellsprings of harmonious living, learning, and leadership that we described at the end of chapter 1. For they are really the bedrock that underlies all of this. If you return to the two parallel diagrams at the beginning of this chapter, you'll note that "collaboration" lies in the same conceptual space as collegial culture of professionalism. For us the link is direct and the message is clear.

There's no way your ELC is going to have a collegial and professionally grounded and oriented culture if you and the rest of your people are not fundamentally and deeply collaborative. Read that as being cooperative, generous, forthright, inclusionary, win-win, team players. Ego only gets in the way of being one of your ELC's generic outcomes: "collaborative contributors." That's what ELCs embody, foster, honor, and thrive on.

But keep looking at the two diagrams because there's more to the message. Since everything in both models is connected to everything else, your ability to be a collaborative contributor is totally connected to your ability to be a contributor, period. And to us this means that being a contributor is the direct result of what you bring to the game and share with your colleagues. It's a product of your consciousness (as we've described it in chapter 1), your creativity, your competence, and your compassion—all interacting with and reinforcing your ability to put those talents and resources out there collaboratively. Why? So that your contribution enhances, expands, elevates, and embellishes those of all your other teammates, and your collective "win" is enlarged manyfold.

This holistic, integrated combination of factors is the key to empowerment, collegiality, and professionalism, and to harmonious learning, leadership, and living. And that's why you'll see it in the second figure at the beginning of every chapter that follows. It's your constant reminder of the "Total" picture.

CHAPTER THREE

CREATING A TRANSFORMATIONAL
PHILOSOPHY AND RATIONALE

As you can see from these two parallel diagrams, the heart, mind, and bedrock of your empowering learning community is its transformational philosophy and rationale. Everything that happens operationally in this systemic model is directly shaped by and aligned with this absolutely critical component. Therefore, it deserves every bit of careful attention you can give it.

The lower diagram shows its counterpart in the *TL2.0* model: authentic leadership. And as we explain in chapter 6 of that book, authentic leaders are the lead learners and lead teachers in their organizations and the champions of shaping organizational values and defining organizational purpose. In a nutshell, they are key to laying the philosophical bedrock of an ELC's "reason" for being everything that it is, and doing everything that it does. This bedrock represents the big, supra answer to the question: Why does your organization exist in its existing form? Our experience suggests that, if framed soundly, your answer will be a composite of four mutually reinforcing, but conceptually distinct, things:

1. Our beliefs—what we assume to be true and good: our paradigm perspective.

2. Our knowledge base—what cutting-edge research indicates is true.

3. Our moral foundation—our core values and principles of professionalism.

Life-Performance
LEARNER OUTCOMES
Aligned
SUPPORT
STRUCTURE
Transformational
PHILOSOPHY
& RATIONALE
Collegial
CULTURE
of Professionalism
Empowering
LEARNING SYSTEM

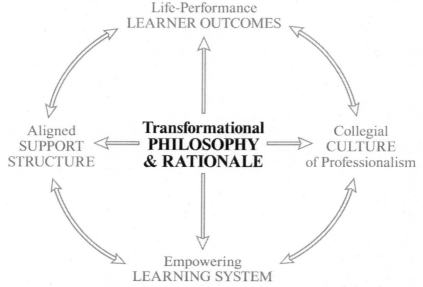

Figure 3.1. Focusing on an ELC's philosophy and rationale.

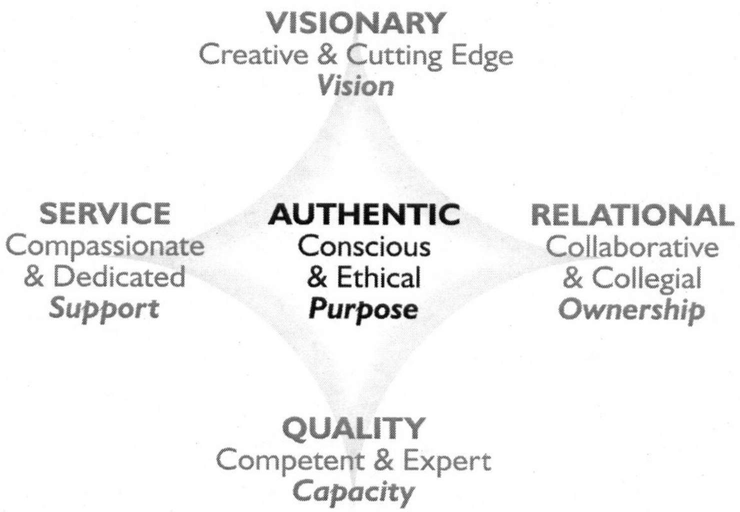

VISIONARY
Creative & Cutting Edge
Vision
SERVICE
Compassionate
& Dedicated
Support
AUTHENTIC
Conscious
& Ethical
Purpose
RELATIONAL
Collaborative
& Collegial
Ownership
QUALITY
Competent & Expert
Capacity

Figure 3.2. The parallel emphasis of Total Leadership 2.0.

4. Our mission/purpose—what we're ultimately here to accomplish.

Our learner outcomes, culture, learning system, and support structure are all direct extensions of these four defining elements, which we consistently use to guide and shape all our decisions, communications, and actions.

And, indeed, all the rest is details. But in this case it's not "the devil" that's in them, it's "the beef" that gives your ELC its meaning, stature, integrity, and reputation. So let's look at each of these four elements carefully, borrowing here and there from key elements we've already described in *Total Leaders 2.0*.

Your ELC's Grounding Beliefs

We cannot tell you what your beliefs are, or should be. Only you and your colleagues know what they are and can bring them to light. All we can do is offer examples and suggestions that may guide you in developing a framework of basic beliefs that you can openly share with all your constituents so that they have no doubt about where you stand and what you stand for. As we offered above, we're equating the term "beliefs" with "assumptions," with "givens," with "filters," with "paradigm perspectives." They are the bedrock of everything you define as true, possible, and good—and tons of research show that you think, decide, and act accordingly.

In chapter 1 we offered two lists of "from–to" ways of viewing educational possibilities, and we encourage you to revisit them to refresh your thinking on this. By presenting those lists we were certainly providing you with some bold contrasts between one configuration of "realities" and another. We called one of them educentrism and the other empowerment. Those labels don't matter as much as whether the kinds of things on one or the other list—or perhaps other things entirely—represent how you fundamentally view

- Learners, their capacities, their intelligences, their potentials, and their interests
- Learning, its basic nature, its processes, and its diverse manifestations
- Learning systems, their essential components, and their empowering features

- Life, expressed in its most natural, most elevating, and most harmonious forms

Whatever your beliefs are about these four things, we encourage you to state them clearly in ways and language everyone can see and understand. Then post them, distribute them, discuss them, and be able to defend and explain them with everyone who is a legitimate constituent of your ELC.

But wait! Don't do it yet. We're going to be addressing some very key things in this chapter that may in fact change/expand/elevate your perspectives on what's really true and possible about learners, learning, learning systems, and life. They may, in fact, take your paradigm back to zero, as we noted in chapter 1. So place a bookmark here, keep reading, and plan to revisit this task once you've reached the end of this chapter.

Expanding Your ELC's Knowledge Base

We didn't always immediately realize it, but every time we had a new insight that really opened up our thinking, we were "going back to zero" in one way or another. That is, our basic assumptions and beliefs about "how things were" got challenged, and we had to expand our knowledge base and rethink things in order to move ahead. And that's all we're asking you to do here. As you consider the exciting possibility of moving from an educentric to a transformational approach to educational change, keep going back to what you really know and keep expanding your understanding of what it means to learn, educate, and live in the age of empowerment.

We're going to highlight five bodies of knowledge here that have dramatically affected our work and have led to *Total Leaders 2.0*, Spady's *Beyond Counterfeit Reforms*, and this book. We're not claiming that this is all you need to consider in creating and implementing a powerful vision for your ELC, but we can assure you that each of the five in its own right has proved to be a powerful eye-opener and paradigm expander for our colleagues across the world. In fact, we've shared what's in the shaded box on the next page countless times on three different continents.

These five age of empowerment knowledge bases are (1) life and its key spheres of living, (2) the future and the conditions that are shaping it, (3) learners and their rich array of capacities and interests, (4) learning

> If humanity had based education on any one of these five knowledge bases, let alone all five together, we'd never have the educentric system we have today!

and its diverse manifestations, and (5) empowered and constructive life performance.

Knowledge Base 1: Life's Spheres of Living

One of our biggest challenges in transcending the educentric paradigm was to realize that the knowledge base called "life" did not match the knowledge base represented in education's traditional curriculum structure. Life is neither focused on nor organized around math, science, social studies, and language arts. The latter are purely "academic constructs"—that is, they are ways of organizing content that reflect the way higher education scholars in the nineteenth century formally divided up areas of research . . . and taught them.

And, in 1893, those rather artificial divisions got built into the recommendations of a highly influential group of educators called "The Committee of Ten," and they've gotten institutionalized, legalized, internalized, legitimated, and reinforced by all of us ever since. We know them as: four years of English, three years of math, three years of science, and so on. Let's face it: They're the bedrock of the educentric paradigm!

So imagine that a century later two fellows named Schwahn and Spady were working with educators across North America urging them to be future focused in their curriculum thinking and to envision quite directly preparing their students for the challenges and conditions they'd be facing after they left the system. We knew that "the world out there" wasn't organized around the subject areas, but we couldn't find any kind of framework that really embodied it. So we invented one! Well, not exactly invented—but we came up with the notion that "life" could be viewed as very fluid, overlapping areas of experience that we soon named "spheres of living."

We were quite tentative about using this concept at first, but after a couple of workshops with a diversity of educational leaders and specialists, it was clear that the concept made great sense to them, and that they could envision organizing a lot of their curriculum around its general themes. In short, their thinking matched ours, and we asked every group—with a few examples and a little coaching—to come up with their best answer to this fundamental strategic design question, shown in the shaded box below.

> If education is supposed to prepare our young people for *life*, what are the key aspects of life (i.e., spheres of living) that they will be engaged with and need to deeply understand?

Over the years educational entities on four continents have grappled with this question and come up with a large array of impressive answers. Here are just a couple of them, to give you a flavor of the richness and diversity of their thinking

Example 1	**Example 2**
Personal potential and wellness	Personal
Learning challenges and resources	Learning
Life and resource management	Culture
Close and significant relationships	Relationships
Group and community memberships	Civic
Work and productive endeavors	Economic
Physical and cultural environment	Global
Purposeful and fulfilling pursuits	

It's interesting that most of the districts/entities that we've worked with chose to represent these spheres in a diagram resembling a daisy, with the first two on these lists represented as concentric circles in the center of the flower, and the other spheres as overlapping petals on the outside. Their intention was to convey the "individual" in the middle, and his or her key spheres of engagement on the outside, with everything ultimately overlapping with everything else.

The "spheres of living" concept has served three key purposes. First, it has really shifted people's paradigms and concept of curriculum content from educentrism to the fundamentals of life experience and how it unfolds. They can readily see that there are tons of good content to teach in each of these spheres that's not addressed in much of their "academic" curriculum.

Second, they can also see that there's a larger and more relevant purpose to curriculum design than is true in many existing subjects. These spheres are literally "where the action is" in people's lives, and the educators we work with readily acknowledge how much students would benefit from consistently engaging with the substance and issues embodied in each. Third, the spheres help educators see that most of what they've been teaching is not an end in itself, but it can be reframed to directly support learning success in each of the spheres.

Please reflect on this spheres concept before moving on. It's a fundamental component of an ELC's transformational knowledge base.

Knowledge Base 2: The Future and Its Powerful Conditions

The second key concept we developed to help educators and their constituents become genuinely future focused came in the form of another key strategic design question posed in the following shaded box.

> If education is supposed to prepare our young people for life, what are the major conditions, challenges, and opportunities they're very likely to face as young adults that they'll need to anticipate and deal with successfully?

This question is intended to compel them to think deeply about what's really happening in the world now, and which shifts and trends are likely to shape the big challenges and opportunities emerging in the foreseeable future.

Chapters 1 and 2 in *TL2.0* contain our version of an extended answer to that question, and we've summarized it in the words: "Welcome to Empowermentland!" and "Living on the Edge in Empowermentland." Those two chapters reflect some high points about both the dynamic, ever-evolving challenge side of life in our ever-evolving age of empowerment, and the opportunities for creative action that exist within every challenge. It's not necessary to repeat or summarize any of that here because you're free to go back and explore those specifics at any time. Instead, we want you to understand the straightforward and powerful why, what, and how of this concept.

For us the purpose of education is to empower and equip all young people with the understandings, skills, and desire to lead fulfilling, contributing lives as young adults and beyond. The key to realizing that purpose, we believe, is having continuous opportunities to learn about, confront, experience, explore, deal with, and even proactively "shape" the conditions/"realities" that they'll be facing once their formal education ends. Some call this "context" learning; for others it's similar to "real-life simulations." Regardless of the name, it represents the ability to apply what you know in theory, or can do in isolation, to the range of settings, situations, and contexts in which you'll be expected to perform competently in real life roles. Furthermore, you learn to master it by doing it—often over and over—across the range of contexts/conditions that you're likely to be facing.

Athletic teams do it constantly; so do all other "performance professionals"—medical personnel, trial lawyers, golfers, musicians, actors, pilots, construction workers, soldiers, et cetera, et cetera, et cetera. It's about coming up against a range of circumstances and being able to execute what you want to do in the face of any, or all, of them.

> Memorizing the manual and passing paper-pencil tests about its content may be necessary first steps for some professionals, but test scores are totally insufficient indicators of versatile and reliable performance.

So for us the message is simple: If this is what our young people will be facing after they leave school, then we'd better give them all the help, exposure, and experience we can while they're with us so they can face those things with confidence and competence—and in all the spheres of living we regard as significant as well. Yes, we are fully aware that this represents a dramatic shift away from the fifteen boxes and educentric paradigm described in chapter 1, but why not? This is what preparing young people for a fulfilling future is all about, and it's why education badly needs authentic leaders to make the argument and ELCs to lead the way.

Knowledge Base 3: Learners and Their Rich Array of Capacities

The educentric paradigm compels us to view young people as "students in school" who have a specific job to do on a specific schedule: Learn the prescribed curriculum! However, we choose to view youngsters through the empowerment lens, as human beings with a rich and amazing array of capacities, "intelligences," interests, and qualities.

This shift adds an incredibly important element to our transformational approach to educational change—something a host of outstanding researchers call being "learner-centered." This transformational paradigm assumes that

> **Almost all children/young people possess a range of**
> **valuable talents and interests that will blossom**
> **if recognized, honored, and cultivated.**

Everything we're describing in this book as promoting empowerment aligns with this viewpoint, and we wish to give full credit to an informal team of outstanding researchers who call themselves the New Possibilities Network for sharing so much of their expertise and wisdom with us over the past few years. In 2007 they developed a set of ten propositions that they call "Timeless Truths about Human Capacity," which for us serve as both the knowledge base and philosophical grounding of learner-centered thinking and practice. As you read and reflect on them, please note how strongly each proposition contrasts with educentrisms's fifteen boxes and represents yet another way of expressing the essence of empowerment.

- Humans are born curious and naturally explore life and their world.

- Humans vary greatly in their rates and ways of learning.

- Humans are born social, and their learning is naturally influenced by others.

- Humans can learn, create, and change throughout their lives.

- Humans naturally use all their senses to learn.

- Humans can take charge of their thoughts and emotions.

- Humans can transcend their current perceived limitations.

- Humans' capacities for intuition, insight, imagination, and creativity are inherent, powerful, and unlimited.

- Humans naturally appreciate and seek to create quality and beauty.

- Humans can naturally access and utilize their innate inner wisdom.

Now that you've read these ten statements about human capacity, we encourage you to strengthen your understanding of each one by pursuing the following five steps. The more often you do them, the more you'll expand your appreciation of the amazing abilities and resilience that we humans possess:

1. Take a deep breath, relax, and read the statements again very slowly, one by one. Really consider what each one portrays and implies.

2. As you read each statement again, think about how it applies to you and how you function in the world. Be sure to highlight the ones that you feel most characterize you and create a kind of profile of yourself—and a profile of others you know well, if that helps.

3. Then read each statement again, but this time think about the kind of learning system that would directly support the kind of capacity being described. Let your thinking range far beyond the fifteen boxes.

4. As you do this third step, ask yourself, "What kind of learning system does this capacity really encourage?" Keep asking yourself the question, and let a picture come together in your mind.

5. Once you've identified some good possibilities, write them down and keep them handy. They're going to be important discussion points as your work with your colleagues and constituents proceeds.

Now, without getting into lots of theory, we'd like you to consider the range and variety of talents, innate abilities, and/or "intelligences" that human beings possess. What are they? Here too we encourage you to make a list of them in your own words. If Howard Gardner's familiar "multiple intelligences" framework comes to mind, start there, but go beyond it. Spady undertook that challenge when he wrote *Beyond Counterfeit Reforms*, and in chapter 3 of that book you'll find the twenty-five he identified. Here they are—just the names. See if you can add others:

Visionary/anticipatory	Social/affiliative
Musical/auditory	Spatial/relational
Verbal/communicative	Mathematical/quantitative
Logical/organizational	Representational/expressive
Openness/receptivity	Recall/associative
Imaginative/creative	Functional/operational
Interpretive/diagnostic	Intuitive/psychic
Conceptual/analytical	Visual/observational
Kinesthetic/physical	Attentiveness/caring
Strategic/systemic	Technical/mechanical
Empathetic/supportive	Selfless/altruistic
Tactile/sensory	Humor/novelty
Gastronomic/olfactory	

Now that you've seen them, we encourage you to take five steps similar to the ones above:

1. Take a deep breath, relax, and read each label again very slowly, one by one, including any new ones you created. Really consider what each one portrays and implies.

2. As before, consider how each of these applies to you personally, and highlight the ones that fit. And as before, create a kind of "multiple intelligences" profile of yourself—and of others you know well too if that helps. Don't be modest, you probably have lots of them. Most people do.

3. Now go back and consider each intelligence again; this time make a list for each one of the people you know or know about who seem to stand out in this way. Then note down how they express their empowerment and contribute to the quality of life in the world by using this intelligence.

4. Then go back through the set of labels again and carefully consider the kinds of life endeavors and careers for which this kind of talent is a major asset. (It may require several sheets of paper for you to do this, but it will be worth the effort as you engage in the design and implementation processes we'll be describing later.)

5. With all of that in hand, go back through the list yet again and think about the kind of learning system that would both honor and foster this particular kind of talent. As before, let your thinking range far beyond the fifteen boxes, and write down your ideas, both now and whenever they might come to you later.

Congratulations! That was a lot to do, but you have just taken a *big* step in expanding the knowledge base for your ELC and shifting its paradigm away from educentrism. Bravo! And we repeat: All of this will become key to the change process you will be initiating. The more often you read through these lists, add to them, discuss them with colleagues, and refine them, the stronger will be your stature as an authentic leader—the lead learner and lead teacher in your organization. And you'll also be strengthening your ability to forge a learner-centered ELC that directly honors and fosters these broad human capacities and more specific intelligences.

Knowledge Base 4: Learning and Its Diverse Manifestations

One of the key limitations of the current "reform" movement in education is its obsession with the term "achievement." It sounds as good as "motherhood and apple pie," everyone "needs" it, and few would dare object to its prime status as the system's operating definition of "learning." Well, we do! And it's why achievement is one of the fifteen boxes in chapter 1. Before you give up on us and think we've gone off the deep end, please consider the following:

1. What's called learning and achievement in today's reform world is a very narrow and limiting slice of the learning pie. It's about the left-brain/cognitive processing of selected content and concepts, period. We call it "one-dimensional learning"—

what people can assimilate/memorize and repeat back on paper-pencil tests. From this educentric perspective, if you're not much of a test-taker you're not going to amount to much in life. (Wrong!)

2. That narrow view of learning overlooks/disregards/diminishes most of the ten statements about human capacity noted above and most of the twenty-five intelligences you just examined. Translation: A vast array of human capacity, intelligence, talent, and potential has become collateral damage in industrial age schools, and it just doesn't count in the eyes of today's educational reformers.

3. The content that students are required to learn has little to do with either the spheres of living or the future conditions that are now part of your ELC's knowledge base. It's content that prepares you for more education in a box, but not for life in Empowermentland!

So what's the essence of the ELC knowledge base regarding learning? Here are two powerful things that you can consistently use to support an empowerment orientation.

First, go back to the list of twenty-five intelligences and look at them as twenty-five ways and kinds of learning. That means that each of us has at least twenty-five ways of processing, internalizing, and applying what we experience, and each of those ways/kinds of learning represents a kind of talent that deserves to be honored and links directly to career success and life fulfillment. Now, if you connect this understanding with what we said in chapter 3 of *TL2.0* about the strengths movement, you'll become an articulate champion for the ELC premise in the shaded box below.

> We all have natural strengths/potentials/intelligences/gifts that make it easier for us to flourish in some aspects of life than others—including leadership.

Why not identify, honor, and build on those strengths, rather than ignore most of them (in the name of educational reform) and force youngsters into one narrow standardized mold that clearly does not work for many of them?

Second, insist on elevating the meaning of learning from "content" to "competence." This means focusing on what learners can actually *do* with what they know. (And, if you want to be daring, also insist that we emphasize *where*—in what contexts—we want the doing to be done and demonstrated.) The key to this is to focus on the verbs that are used in defining learning expectations/outcomes/standards. If you see a lot of verbs like *know* and *understand*, you're dealing with cognitive processing. But if you see what English teachers call "action verbs"—like *design*, *illustrate*, *negotiate*, *produce*, and *create*—you're much closer to real competence, and that's where we want you and your ELC to be. Moreover, you can't legitimately assess action verbs like these with paper-pencil testing— "authentic" demonstrations are required—which is another stake in the heart of educentrism!

Knowledge Base 5: Empowered and Constructive Life Performance

This fifth critical ELC knowledge base actually lies at the intersection of the previous four. It's where we connect the "life-grounding" and "future-focusing" elements of 1 and 2 with the "learners and learning" elements of 3 and 4. The concept that emerged for us nearly twenty years ago is known as "life performance." In some of its manifestations it's also known as "life-role performers." It's our response to the critical strategic design question in the box below.

> If this is the kind of society we wish to create/preserve, then what kind of human beings do we want our education system to send out the door?

Based on what we've presented so far in this chapter, it's easy to simply say: "fully empowered humans equipped to lead fulfilling, contributing lives as young adults and beyond." Yes, that provides an empowering grounding for our work, but what does this really look like? What can we say more specifically about their qualities and abilities? Here, as briefly as we can describe it, is our three-part answer for now. There will be much more analysis of this whole issue in the next chapter.

First, let's elaborate a little on what we just said about competence. It's the ability to *do* something consistently and well. Fine, but we learned early on in our work that "doing" takes many forms—from very small, specific, defined tasks to incredibly large, complex, open-ended undertakings. It's rather like laying bricks on the one hand, and designing and building a cathedral on the other. (A much fuller explanation of this is provided in chapter 10 of *Beyond Counterfeit Reforms*, and we encourage you to add it to your knowledge base as well.)

Second, without elaborating more on that particular point, let's assume that the two most complex forms of doing are called "performance roles" and "life-role performances" respectively. They both embody complex configurations of abilities (the twenty-five intelligences) that people can carry out across a range of content areas and context challenges. In other words, role performers are both competent and versatile! The words *mediator, coach, communicator, learner, designer, problem solver,* and *producer* illustrate the variety of important performance roles all of us step into at one time or another as functioning adults. As you can see, they're not occupational titles; they're the complex functions we carry out within our "life-role" called "occupation"—or our other life-roles, called "parent," "citizen," "family member," and so on.

Third, let's also assume that the strategic question posed above could be answered in role-performance language, which is what happened "by accident" for the first time in a Colorado school district in early 1991. The district was engaged in an early version of our strategic design process, and its people wanted to create a future-focused vision of the kind of human beings they were committed to "sending out the door," regardless of the conventional boxes and labels that defined their system.

The framework that emerged from their intensive process still holds up remarkably well nearly two decades later against our contemporary definition of empowerment. In so many words, they said:

> Regardless of their GPA, courses taken, program area, sex, age, or ethnicity, we want every student who leaves our system to step into their future as a: Self-Directed Learner, Collaborative Worker, Complex Thinker, Community Contributor, and Quality Producer.

In addition, their strategic design process also implied: "and we have to transform our curriculum and how we teach to ensure that that happens

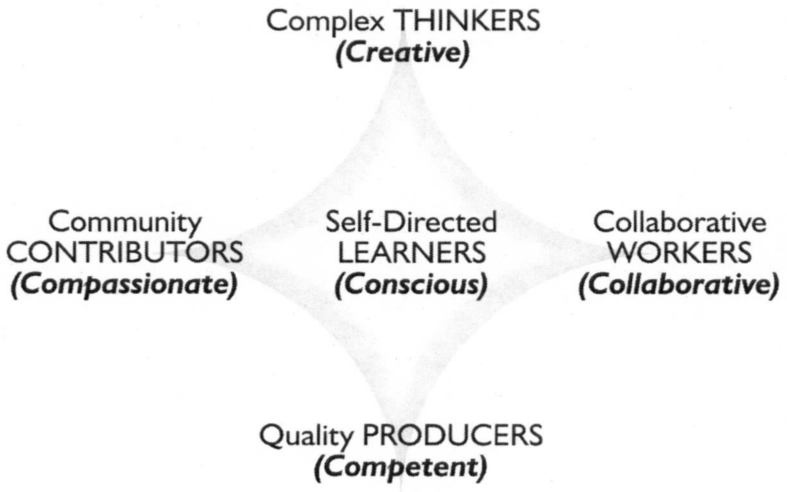

Complex THINKERS
(Creative)

Community | Self-Directed | Collaborative
CONTRIBUTORS | LEARNERS | WORKERS
(Compassionate) | *(Conscious)* | *(Collaborative)*

Quality PRODUCERS
(Competent)

Figure 3.3. Connecting life performance outcomes with the five well-springs.

for all of them!" Please read this longer statement again. It's remarkably close to what we're hoping your ELC will soon be able to assert.

Moreover, it has struck us over the years that this framework happens to map pretty closely on the five wellsprings that the *TL2.0* model embodies. Note the parallels in figure 3.3.

What a remarkable paradigm shift this framework represented when it was first created—not only because their statement of what came to be called "exit outcomes" transcended the conventional fifteen boxes, but especially because it was, to our knowledge, the first outcomes framework ever to be formally expressed in "human" terms. Yes, everyone present, from kindergarten teachers to school board members to the high school students on the design team, could envision children of all ages being and demonstrating these five things. For example, five-year-olds, ten-year-olds, and sixteen-year-olds could all be self-directed learners. The only difference would be the level of maturity/complexity at which this would be demonstrated.

Remember, we'll be adding lots of detail to this, particularly in chapter 4, but it's worth going over this Colorado district's framework again and again. It stands out as addressing so many vital abilities in so few words.

Status Check

At the beginning of this chapter we said that this component of your ELC is literally its philosophical bedrock. Your ELC's beliefs, knowledge base, moral foundation, and purpose together provide the declared "reason" that you exist and what you stand for. So far we've looked at two of those four elements, with two more to go. We've devoted a lot of space to expanding your knowledge base because we think it's a key to: (1) opening up your grounding beliefs/paradigm perspective, (2) coming to see and value things differently, and (3) expanding your sense of mission and purpose.

Once we address the final two of these elements, you'll have our perspective on an ELC's transformational philosophy and rationale. If you stick to our strategic design process, it, then, will become the definer and driving force of everything else your ELC does. We don't again need to list all your ELC's components here to make the point; just look at the diagram at the beginning of the chapter. The whole story is there in very few words.

Establishing Your ELC's Moral Foundation

Your personal moral foundation is the key to your credibility and trust as a leader. We address that twice in *TL2.0*: first near the end of chapter 3, then as a key aspect of authentic leadership in chapter 6. Your ELC's moral foundation is a critical part of its organizational culture, and we just explained why and how in chapter 2 by focusing extensively on the concept of professionalism. Now we're back again with yet more on your ELC's moral foundation, this time to add another layer to the cake and put frosting on it as well.

In one sense, morality, culture, and paradigm thinking—which often include religion—are inseparable. In one culture, if you do something considered wrong, they may lash you with a whip. In another, if you do the same thing, they send you to jail—no whipping allowed. In another, the same offense gets you psychological counseling, period. And in another, they may ignore it altogether.

No, we're not making an argument here for what some call "moral relativism." We're just pointing out that what is seen as wrong, offensive, obscene, or inappropriate in one social or cultural setting is viewed/

interpreted/dealt with quite differently in another. Or turn that around: The meanings and manifestations of good, honorable, admirable, or appropriate vary greatly as well. The constant factor here, as we explained in chapter 2, is that groups can have enormous sanctioning or approval power over their members—and lots of it is subtle/informal.

Universal Core Values

When we focus on values, morals, principles, and norms in "modern"/ Western societies and organizations, however, there's a lot more agreement about the things people believe deserve collective approval, and the things that deserve sanctioning. Our study of the leadership literature of the past twenty years or so suggests, in fact, that there are a number of what we'll call core values that receive nearly universal approval. The list is quite large, so we've worked pretty extensively with the ten that we found were endorsed/embraced most often.

As you review and reflect on them, think about how significant each is to how you would want an *empowering* learning *community* (notice our emphasis) to function if you were a student there. What criteria/ priorities would you want guiding the behavior and decisions of the adults in that organization? And what values would you want them fostering and modeling for their students? You might want to revise our definitions a bit, but keep both the spirit and the substance of each value in mind as you reflect on it.

- **Integrity**. The long-term expression and embodiment of honesty, fairness, trustworthiness, honor, and consistent adherence to high-level principles, especially those recognized and endorsed by one's organization.

- **Courage**. The willingness of individuals and organizations to risk themselves despite the likelihood or perception of negative consequences, or fear of the unknown.

- **Honesty**. Being fully transparent, candid, and truthful, while being sensitive to the thoughts, needs, and feelings of others.

- **Reflection**. The process of using a values screen to review, assess, and evaluate decisions you and your organization have made or will make, and the actions you and your organization have taken or will take.

- **Commitment**. People's willingness to devote their full energies and talents to the successful completion of undertakings they have agreed to pursue, despite challenges and adverse conditions that may arise.

- **Productivity**. The optimum use of available time, resources, technologies, and talent to achieve desired results.

- **Teamwork**. Working collaboratively and cooperatively toward achieving a common recognized end, with individuals going out of their way to make the performance or results of others easier and better.

- **Openness**. Grounded in a sense of psychological security, it reflects a willingness and desire to receive, consider, and act ethically on information, possibilities, and perspectives of all kinds.

- **Excellence**. A desire for, and pursuit of, the highest quality in any undertaking, process, product, or result.

- **Risk Taking**. Extending beyond the tried, true, and familiar to do different things a different way, often without the assurance of success. It embodies taking initiative, innovating, and speaking out.

When we work with organizations to develop their moral foundation, we also include a parallel concept: principles of professionalism—those ethical standards of decision making and performance that transcend personal considerations and circumstantial pressures to promote the higher good of the organization and its clients. We worked with these ten principles in the latter half of chapter 2, and we encourage you to review them there and give them the same analysis that you just did with the core values.

Basic Steps for Creating a Collective Moral Foundation

Here's the place where you share your personal perspectives about these values and principles with your colleagues and collectively commit yourselves to a key set of each that will become "non-negotiable" standards to which your ELC's members are all committed. We've developed a simple process for carrying out this analysis that has worked successfully with a number of leadership teams, and we encourage you to follow it, or something similar. The five steps below will enable you collectively to be intentional about your moral foundation and to go on record with its key elements, what they will look like in action, and how you intend to monitor them.

1. Discuss the core values and the principles of professionalism here and in chapter 2 so that everyone understands the definition, deeper meaning, and intention of each.

2. As a group, thoughtfully and deliberately identify the three or so core values and the three or so principles of professionalism that, if acted upon effectively, would move your team/organization toward functioning consistently as a value- and principle-driven one. (Identifying fewer key values and principles allows for sharper focus and improves the chances that they will be consistently embodied in your decisions and actions.)

3. Candidly and boldly identify two or three behaviors that you will commit to doing for each of the priority values and principles you selected, and two or three behaviors that you will stop doing for each of them. Be candid about this and make statements about significant things that are easy to identify. For instance, if one of your priorities is the core value of openness, one of your "will stop doing" statements might be: "We will stop saying things in the parking lot that we didn't have the courage to say at the meeting."

4. Determine how your team will monitor its progress in implementing these moral foundation priorities. For instance, you may end each meeting with a discussion of how you are doing on one specific value or principle. You might add meaning to the discussion by rotating the responsibility for leading that discussion, and you may want the person responsible for that particular meeting to take the group through some type of

activity to dramatize the definition of that specific value or principle.

5. Determine how you might deal with individual members who continually speak and act inconsistently with your key values or principles. You may choose one of the alternatives noted earlier (whipping, jail, counseling, public humiliation, etc.— just kidding) or hold a one-on-one intervention with them.

When this process is complete, you'll be ready to address the fourth and final element in your moral foundation, your ELC's mission/purpose.

Creating a Compelling Purpose for Your ELC

An organization's compelling purpose virtually drives everything else it does because it declares its "reason for being." If an organization lacks one, anyone can justify focusing their attention and energies on just about anything, and they won't be wrong for doing so. There's no clear direction or priority to guide them other than their own preferences, and that leads to disarray or worse.

Our extensive analysis of the leadership and change literature as well as our personal experiences indicate that effective, dynamic, and enduring organizations

- Have a clear and compelling purpose that they involve all stake-holders in creating, implementing, and maintaining

- Embody the values and paradigm perspectives of the staff in defining that purpose

- Align all organizational functions and decisions with that purpose

When an organization has a compelling purpose, everyone knows where it and its people are headed. The purpose helps everyone determine what they should be doing, and equally important, tells them what they can stop doing. Whoa! Stop! Read that one again. It's a blockbuster: "and equally important, tells them what they can stop doing"—for example, the routines and rituals that surround the fifteen boxes mentioned in chapter 2.

We believe that an organization's purpose statement (some equate it with being their mission) should be very brief, hard-hitting, dynamic, and direction-setting. Our rule of thumb is expressed below:

**If it's over ten words, you've got an essay,
not a purpose statement.**

And if it's an essay, people have to find it and read it to remember it. That's profoundly less compelling and direction-setting than having it on the tip of your tongue and the front of your mind.

The good ones we've seen in education usually contain the words "all students" and focus on equipping them for the complex future they face. However, the best one we've ever seen comes from Federal Express, and we'd love to have you come up with something as creative and compelling. Ready? Here it is: "10:30!" It's hard to be more compelling, dynamic, hard-hitting, direction setting, and brief than that, and it's certainly on the tip of every employee's tongue and in the front of their minds, too! Wow, what a zinger.

As we noted earlier, three things will underlie your purpose statement: your paradigm perspectives, your knowledge base, and your moral foundation. Let's just consider them to be your ELC's rationale. The more explicit, detailed, and soundly reasoned these three rationale elements are, the more likely it is that your statement will withstand "the slings and arrows of outrageous fortune" that may come your way from diehard skeptics. So please get them firmly in place first, then be prepared to say as we did at the beginning of the chapter:

1. These are our *beliefs*—what we assume to be true and good: our paradigm perspective

2. This is our *knowledge base*—what cutting edge research indicates is true

3. This is our *moral foundation*—our core values and principles of professionalism

Then note that your "real" purpose will take two forms. The first is the brief, hard-hitting statement we've been mentioning. This statement is more than a catchy phrase you can put on your school or district stationery, newsletters, or bumper stickers. They're the words that frame and shape your decision-screen for what's important and honored, and what isn't appropriate or allowed, in your organization. Typically this statement should start with a powerful action verb that immediately conveys your intention. *Empower*, *equip*, and *ensure* are three strong ones. And they're likely to be followed by "all students." That leaves you with seven more, so choose them carefully.

And please note: Not only are the words you select extremely important, but so is what you make of them. For example, if your purpose is "enabling *all* students to succeed in a challenging world," then you should stop grading them on the bell curve because it implies that some must do poorly while others succeed.

The second form your purpose will take is the framework of life performance learner outcomes you'll be deriving for your ELC. They transform your short statement of intent into a tangible, dynamic, compelling expression of the results you're there to achieve, and we'll be addressing them next. Many districts make this link by including a preamble to their learner outcomes framework that says:

We will know we are accomplishing our mission/purpose when all of our students leave our schools as . . .

Then follows the wording of their outcomes framework, for example: self-directed learners, collaborative workers, complex thinkers, community contributors, and quality producers.

Sound familiar? Well, keep reading, because chapter 4 provides numerous inspiring examples from schools or districts across the world from which you are welcome to draw inspiration, ideas, and words.

CHAPTER FOUR
DERIVING LIFE-PERFORMANCE LEARNER OUTCOMES

At the end of chapter 1 we noted that this component of your empowering learning community might represent the greatest of all paradigm-shifting challenges to your colleagues and constituents. That's why we devoted so much time in chapter 3 to describing the kind of knowledge base you will need to carry out this exciting process successfully. And it's also why we opened the door to this topic both there and in chapter 1. The more time and attention you can give to this new way of thinking about and working with the life-performance nature of learner outcomes, the more transformational and genuinely empowering your ELC will be.

Challenging Most of the Key Boxes

The significance of this component has been clear to us for the two-plus decades that we've been collaborating. Whether you're explicit about them or not, your outcomes are the products/ends/results of your instructional efforts. And as we'll be repeating later in the chapter, they embody what your students will be taking with them when they "walk out the door" and exit the system on graduation night. For us they're the real "why"/reason/purpose that your organization exists—just like getting packages to customers before 10:30 is Federal Express's.

Hence, the choice you face is whether to define what you want your vision of an empowered and successful learner to be before you start— and explicitly align your learning system and support structure with that

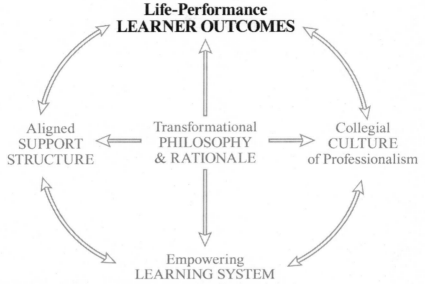

Life-Performance LEARNER OUTCOMES

Aligned SUPPORT STRUCTURE

Transformational PHILOSOPHY & RATIONALE

Collegial CULTURE of Professionalism

Empowering LEARNING SYSTEM

Figure 4.1.   Focusing on an ELC's learner outcomes.

VISIONARY
Creative & Cutting Edge
Vision

SERVICE
Compassionate
& Dedicated
Support

AUTHENTIC
Conscious
& Ethical
Purpose

RELATIONAL
Collaborative
& Collegial
Ownership

QUALITY
Competent & Expert
Capacity

Figure 4.2.   The parallel emphasis of Total Leadership 2.0.

vision—or teach as best you can and see what your learners look like when they exit your system.

From the very first time that we derived/created a life-performance outcomes framework with the Colorado district mentioned in chapter 3, the people who saw that framework immediately and enthusiastically—and surprisingly, we might add—embraced it. For the first time in their careers they could see that (1) learning and learning results could be expressed in a way that really focused on the learner as a human being, (2) learners of all ages and abilities could readily experience success in developing and demonstrating these life-relevant abilities, and (3) outcomes such as these would simultaneously liberate both educators and students from the major constraints of at least twelve of education's fifteen educentric boxes:

- The Curriculum Subjects B☐X
- The Requirements B☐X
- The Time/Schedule B☐X
- The Grade Level B☐X
- The IQ B☐X
- The Achievement B☐X
- The Standards B☐X
- The Test Score B☐X
- The Opportunity B☐X
- The Program/Tracking B☐X
- The Classroom B☐X
- The Role/Control B☐X

So while these twelve boxes are still in front of us, let's emphasize this critical point. If your ELC declared—like that Colorado district did in 1991—that its "real" outcomes for its learners was to have every one of them step out into the future as . . .

Self-Directed Learners   Collaborative Workers   Complex Thinkers
Community Contributors   Quality Producers

. . . then which of these twelve boxes would you want to retain in its traditional educentric form to assure that this happened? We think the answer is "None of them."

Wow! Think about it. Change one key component of a school, and the logical justification for keeping almost all of its educentric/industrial age/assembly-line structural constraints in place melts away. Now that's either profoundly exciting or profoundly scary, depending on which side of the paradigm coin you're operating from. But when this first happened in early 1991, literally every North American school district that we shared this framework with during that period got excited about it and wanted to "borrow" (steal) it. After we explained that they had to create their own in order to establish local ownership and commitment for it, they all willingly agreed to do so—and with a sense of both urgency and excitement, as if they wanted to make up for a century or so of lost time.

Rethinking the Basics

In order to proceed successfully with this innovative, future-focused, learner-centered task, every participating entity had to go through a brief but rigorous orientation process that helped them transcend the constraints of each of the twelve boxes above. Its intent was to liberate them from one-dimensional thinking about learning to what we called a three-dimensional model that involved (1) content and concepts, (2) competence in its more complex forms, and (3) "context" learning and demonstrations—people carrying out complex performance roles in a variety of demanding settings and situations.

We summarized this in chapter 3 in the section called "Knowledge Base 5," and we urge you to revisit that discussion rather than repeat it here. Nonetheless, here are the critical basics that you must keep in mind if you're to pursue what follows with the integrity it requires:

1. Competence is the ability to *do* something, not simply to know/understand it.

2. The nature of the competence/skill/ability is determined by the "action" verb that defines it. ("Negotiate" means negotiate, and "construct" means construct—not simply knowing and understanding things about negotiating and constructing.)

These verbs take learning to the second dimension—beyond the cognitive processing of content alone.

3. Very few, if any, action verbs can be accurately assessed using conventional paper-pencil testing and scoring methods.

4. Competence varies enormously, from the simple and specific (i.e., finite tasks) to the complex and general—what we call performance roles and life roles. The direct expectation here is that teachers must "teach" these action verbs/processes, and learners must be able to execute/demonstrate them over an extended period of time, and across a range of content.

5. Since all "doing" happens "somewhere" (learning and performance contexts—the third dimension in the learning process), the complexity and challenges embedded in these contexts dramatically affect the depth and complexity of the competence required.

6. The more diverse and complex the contexts are, the higher the level of competence must be, and the longer the learning/experience path must be for it to develop and mature. Complex competences take many years to develop—not days or weeks.

Again, the more time you can spend reflecting on the meaning and implications of these six propositions, the better. And we're confident that you'll come to see why they break down the conventional way in which the twelve boxes above are defined and used in educentric practice. If you want examples, think high-level athletic, musical, dramatic, or piloting performance. It takes *many* years of focused practice and development across a range of challenging contexts to become a true master or expert at these and countless other life-performance roles. And yes, there are identifiable stepping-stones along the way in all of these cases because the model is one of consistent long-term growth and improvement, not short-term memorization of information.

Hence, as the participants in that original Colorado district immediately realized, being a self-directed learner happens at ever-evolving levels of complexity throughout a child's and person's life, starting before they even reach school. It's not something taught as a unit or a course during their career. In fact, if the truth be known, one of the participants in the original design group stunned his colleagues with the following observation, shown in the box below:

> When our students enter school at age five, they're already self-directed learners, collaborative workers, complex thinkers, community contributors, and quality producers. The problem is we turn them into "students," and by fourth grade they aren't any of those things any more.
>
> —a Colorado administrator, 1991

Yes, he really got the message, and his paradigm perspective had gone back to zero. And, in less than a minute, his bold statement simply brought all of his colleagues back there with him.

Most "Outcomes" Aren't Really Outcomes

We think one of the biggest challenges you might face in this process relates to the term "outcomes" itself. The great paradox and challenge here is that most of the ones being touted by today's educentric reformers aren't outcomes at all. At best they're curriculum objectives—goals that are taken from the existing curriculum, labeled as "outcomes," and then used as "standards" for judging student learning.

Whew! That's a lot to process for one short paragraph. But that's where we ourselves were over twenty years ago with outcomes, and it's where almost everyone still is today—mired in the fifteen boxes and what we call "the CBO syndrome":

> curriculum-based outcomes . . . content-bound objectives . . . calendar-based opportunities . . . convenience-based operations . . . convention-bound orientations . . . et cetera.

It's all about the boxes, and it took us years to eventually work/crawl/think/design our way out. So here's our take on the learner outcomes picture in five key points that expand on much of what we just said about three-dimensional learning:

1. Outcomes are "culminating demonstrations of learning." This means that learners must actually *do* something that is visible/ observable at or after the end of a significant learning experience. And, as we just noted, the nature of that demonstration is going to be heavily determined by the action verb or verbs used to define the outcome. Hence, "develop" really means develop, and "design" means design. All action verbs require aligned/"authentic" assessments, so choose your verbs carefully.

2. At or after the *real* end doesn't occur every Friday, or at the end of each six weeks, or the end of each semester, or every June. The real end occurs when learners exit the system. Everything before that is "learning opportunity" time and a stepping-stone toward that culmination time—when everything comes together and when learners ultimately leave the system. That's why the genuine culminating ones that we're addressing here have been known for twenty years as "exit outcomes."

3. Demonstrations can take many forms. The micro ones are small tasks and skills. The significant ones are complex demonstrations involving multiple kinds of abilities. They're the ones adults are expected to perform every day in their career, family, civic, and recreational life-roles. We call them "role performance outcomes" and those who can demonstrate them consistently (using a range of content and concepts in a variety of settings and circumstances) are called "role performers."

4. To become good/adept at anything requires lots of exposure, experience, and practice. The complex abilities involved in becoming an adept/versatile role performer take many years to develop and refine. They're not learned out of a book or in a one-shot segment of curriculum. Their essence is experiential and applied—not simply cognitive—and they generally require tons of EQ, not just IQ.

5. All outcomes have a grounding or "base"—they come from somewhere and inherently lead somewhere. The educentric

ones are derived from the curriculum; others appear to emerge out of thin air (i.e., people just make them up). The ones identified here are derived from the spheres of living, future conditions, wellsprings, and moral foundation described in chapter 3. The curriculum ones lead to yet more curriculum, from whence they came. The life-performance (LP) ones lead to more/better life performance. We view the curriculum ones as enabling elements of some of the LPs. They're not ends in themselves.

As you've probably noticed, we've just compressed over two decades of work into a very few pages, and we're now ready to move to the outcome-deriving process itself. It too will be very focused, but we've already laid the groundwork for you in our entire chapter 3 discussion of the knowledge base that underlies an ELC. So please take the time to refresh yourself on those five key elements before proceeding. It will help all of what follows make a lot more sense.

Key Steps in the Outcome-Deriving Process

We're going to assume that you have extended a broad invitation to all of your ELC's constituents/stakeholders to participate in this vision-creating phase of the strategic design process. The key decision you'll have to make at this point concerns the questions you're going to ask them to address that will enable you to derive/generate a powerful and compelling framework of life-performance learner outcomes. Hint: You don't want to pull your outcomes out of thin air because you ultimately won't be able to explain or defend them. And you know they don't emanate out of the traditional curriculum, or you'd end up with educentric ones. The other reasonable option is the grounding of this book: Empowermentland! It's where we all live, and where our futures will unfold.

Creating Your "Spheres of Living" Framework

But on this visit to Empowermentland, we're going to ask our constituents to answer a slightly different version of the question we posed in chapter 3. It's posed in the box below.

If our learning community is supposed to prepare our young people for life in Empowermentland, what are the key spheres of living that they'll be engaged with there, need to be prepared for, and deeply understand?

Immediately after posing this question, you'll need to be ready to "prime the pump" a bit by showing them examples of what these spheres might be. The two frameworks in chapter 3 are excellent starting points and will surely stimulate a lot of fruitful analysis of what life is really all about and what today's learners need to prepare for. Here they are again, just to make this step easier for you:

Spheres Framework 1
Personal potential and wellness
Learning challenges and resources
Life and resource management
Close and significant relationships
Group and community memberships
Work and productive endeavors
Physical and cultural environment
Purposeful and fulfilling pursuits

Spheres Framework 2
Personal
Learning
Culture
Relationships
Civic
Economic
Global

We think it's very important here to keep your people focused on the spheres themselves, not all the change conditions that will be coming up in a moment. Your outcome here is a framework of the spheres that you consider most significant for your learners to fully comprehend and participate in constructively. It can be one of these two frameworks if either appeals to you, some combination of the two, or other related things expressed in your own words. The precise number of spheres you identify doesn't matter, but most workable frameworks range between seven and nine. If you get to ten, please put on the brakes and see if you can do some consolidating.

Developing Your Future Conditions Framework

Your second strategic question will really open the door to deep and lengthy discussion, and you should allow for it in your strategic design schedule. Here it is again in the box below, also in modified form.

> If our learning community is supposed to prepare our young people for life in Empowermentland, what are the major conditions, challenges, and opportunities they're very likely to face there as young adults that they'll need to anticipate and deal with successfully?

Again, you'll need to be ready to prime the pump, but this time with some kind of condensed version of what's in chapters 1 and 2 of *TL2.0*, supplemented with other appropriate material. Clearly there are tons of things to consider here, so it might be wise to poll your group to see if they'd like to answer this question in general terms, or sphere by sphere, as some entities have done.

If you choose the latter alternative, there should be a separate discussion group for each sphere, and the group should focus its answers accordingly. But in either case, you'll need to break people into workable discussion groups and have a way of pooling and consolidating their answers into what you could call your "future conditions framework." This framework, as well as your spheres one, will serve as the bedrock for the final stages of your outcome-deriving process, so take your time with it, make it concrete, and be prepared to share it widely with all your ELC's constituents.

Forging a Profile of Learner Attributes

The third and final element we'd like you to establish as part of your rock-solid/bulletproof rationale for your framework of life-performance learner outcomes is a profile of key learner attributes that you seek to honor and cultivate in your ELC. This profile will embody a combination of three different things discussed in chapter 3: (1) the knowledge base concerning learners and their rich array of capacities, (2) your moral foundation of core values and principles of professionalism, and (3) the five wellsprings of harmonious living, learning, and leadership.

If you want to put a label on it, this will be your statement of the "character" (broadly interpreted) that you want your learners to embody as they step out into their individual futures. And, as you'll see in a moment, these attributes will be very important elements in the outcome-deriving process that follows.

Deriving Your ELC's Framework of Life-Performance Outcomes

Ta-da! Now you're finally ready for the *big one*—the question that you'll be using to derive your life-performance outcomes framework. But as you ask it, and as your people begin to answer it, you're going to have to bring virtually everything you've considered and done so far front and center—probably on poster paper lining the walls of your working area, including

1. Your beliefs and paradigm perspectives, your knowledge bases about learners and life-performance, your core values and principles, and your organizational purpose statement—all from the key elements in your transformational philosophy and rationale

2. Your spheres of living, future conditions, and learner profile frameworks, and explanations and examples of life-performance outcomes frameworks (to prime the pump)

Here's the question, in the following shaded box:

> If this is the future our young people are facing, and these are the inherent capacities they possess, and these are the things we deeply value, then what kind of human beings do we want to send out the door at graduation time with strong confidence in their success?

Listed below are several examples of how that question (or a very similar one) has been answered by public, private, and parochial entities in different parts of the world. However, we're going to present them in two different groupings. The first group shows the results from groups that were either broadly or quite specifically focused on the spheres of living as their key grounding point. These frameworks usually contain between seven and nine life-performance outcomes. The second set of frameworks come from entities that were using the five wellsprings as their major frame of reference. We'll say more about them shortly.

79

Please note that in almost all cases the "role performer" words in each framework are represented in all capital letters, and their modifiers—what we call their "qualitative attributes"—are lowercase. This is a stylistic convention, but it's not a "rule" you have to apply. Our initial thinking was that the role performer words were the real definers of the outcome and needed to be emphasized. We've simply stayed with that notion over the years.

Note also the variation in formats. Some use single words for each; others contain up to two words for each. There's no hard and fast rule on this either, but our own thinking on the matter evolved from the "one of each" to the "two of each" alternative over time. What you'll see in those cases is that the role performer words are pretty closely related, but the qualitative attributes complement each other. For example, since every word really counts, saying "cheerful" and "friendly" is essentially repetitive, so we urge our clients not to "waste" words.

Frameworks Based on the Spheres of Living

Please consider the insight and depth of thinking that underlies the following four examples, how expansive these educators' visions about learners, learning, and life are, and how different our world would be if visions like these guided the world's education systems:

Self-directed LEARNERS	Self-actualizing PERSONS	Empowering FRIENDS
Involved CITIZENS	Caring STEWARDS	Quality PRODUCERS
	Enlightened CONTRIBUTORS	

Listeners and Communicators	Learners and Thinkers	Leaders and Organizers
Teachers and Mentors	Mediators and Facilitators	Team Players and Supporters
Investigators and Problem Solvers	Innovators and Creators	Performers and Contributors

(No qualitative attributes in this otherwise rich example)

Purposeful, self-directed, adaptable . . .

LEARNERS and MENTORS

CREATORS and
CONTRIBUTORS

ORGANIZERS and
FACILITATORS

PROBLEM SOLVERS and
INNOVATORS

LISTENERS and
COMMUNICATORS

THINKERS and
INVESTIGATORS

TEAM PLAYERS and
SUPPORTERS

MEDIATORS and
NEGOTIATORS

LEADERS and IMPLEMENTERS

Self-directed, inquisitive LEARNERS and THINKERS

Ethical, versatile COMMUNICATORS and NEGOTIATORS

Imaginative, discerning RESEARCHERS and
PROBLEM SOLVERS

Visionary, trustworthy LEADERS and MOTIVATORS

Adept, resilient INNOVATORS and PRODUCERS

Responsive, supportive PARTICIPANTS and COLLABORATORS

Thoughtful, global CITIZENS and CONTRIBUTORS

As you read, reread, and reflect on these four frameworks, do your best to put yourself in the shoes of those people just like yourself who generated them. They willingly rose to an incredible opportunity: creating a completely non-educentric version of their organization's mission/purpose/reason for existing. That purpose is learner centered, future focused, fully empowering, and uniquely expressed in human terms—not as curriculum content or specific skills.

Moreover, their intention in describing these powerful outcomes is for them to apply to all students of all ages in all stages of their educational experience—five-year-olds, ten-year-olds, thirteen-year-olds, and seventeen-year-olds, all being practiced and demonstrated at levels of complexity and maturity suitable to their age and level of development. Hence, a profound transformation in how they, and you, educate in the age of empowerment.

Frameworks Based on the Five Wellsprings

Once the five wellsprings of learning, living, and leading had emerged from the continuing evolution of the original Total Leaders model, a variety of educators in different parts of the world recognized their transformational potential and chose to work with them quite explicitly. In several cases in North America, Australia, and South Africa, they chose to derive life-performance learner outcomes from them as extensions of their focus on the spheres of living and future conditions.

Several of these frameworks are provided below, including those from alternative schools that, as you will see in the latter examples, are quite unconstrained in recognizing the deep inner/spiritual nature of humans and fostering it in their ELCs. In each case the elements in these frameworks follow the same sequence: conscious, creative, collaborative, competent, and compassionate.

Informed, reflective PERSONS
Inquisitive, visionary INNOVATORS
Ethical, responsive PARTNERS
Adept, productive PERFORMERS
Caring, community CONTRIBUTORS

Self-directed, thoughtful LEARNERS and PERSONS
Eclectic, creative THINKERS and INNOVATORS
Adept, versatile COMMUNICATORS and COLLABORATORS
Visionary, enterprising IMPLEMENTERS and PERFORMERS
Discerning, global STEWARDS and CONTRIBUTORS

Reflective, self-directed DEVELOPING PROFESSIONALS
Imaginative, insightful OPPORTUNITY CREATORS
Reliable, supportive TEAM MEMBERS
Competent, informed EMERGING PROFESSIONALS
Responsible, contributing COMMUNITY PARTICIPANTS

Prudent, organized LIFE MANAGERS, guided by an ethos of
reflection and improvement

Resourceful, entrepreneurial OPPORTUNITY CREATORS
. . . initiative and innovation

Active, collaborative CITIZENS, guided by an ethos of honesty and
reliability

Skilled, productive CONTRIBUTORS, guided by an ethos of
diligence and quality

Conscientious, global STEWARDS, guided by an ethos of caring and
commitment

Healthy, confident LEARNERS and PLAYERS

Imaginative, versatile EXPLORERS and INNOVATORS

Respectful, supportive COMMUNICATORS and PARTNERS

Self-directed, resourceful CREATORS and PERFORMERS

Caring, responsible CONTRIBUTORS and STEWARDS

Empowered, ethical HUMANS

Eclectic, visionary THINKERS and INNOVATORS

Respectful, responsible COMMUNICATORS and TEAM
MEMBERS

Resourceful, responsible IMPLEMENTERS and PERFORMERS

Ethical, spiritual BEINGS and ADVOCATES

Visionary, resilient EXPLORERS and PROBLEM SOLVERS

Receptive, collaborative PARTNERS and MENTORS

Adept, productive PERFORMERS and IMPLEMENTERS

Discerning, compassionate STEWARDS and CONTRIBUTORS

Unique, loving SPIRITUAL BEINGS

Visionary, innovative EXPLORERS and INVENTORS

Heartfelt, trustworthy COMMUNICATORS and MENTORS

Joyful, talented PERFORMERS and MANIFESTORS

Forthright, global LEADERS and STEWARDS

Aware, reflective SPIRITUAL BEINGS, developing their conscious
identity and inner growth

Visionary, resourceful EXPLORERS and INNOVATORS,
developing their creative imaginations to the fullest

Supportive, trustworthy TEAM PLAYERS and MENTORS,
developing their collaborative interactions with others

Versatile, productive PERFORMERS and IMPLEMENTERS,
developing their competent implementation abilities

Active, global CONTRIBUTORS and STEWARDS, developing their
compassionate involvement with the world

As in the previous examples, there is an enormous amount to absorb and reflect on in these nine frameworks, and we encourage you to do so. But we'd like to call your special attention to the fourth one because it is the most fully developed version of the process that we have yet facilitated. It is actually a simulation meticulously developed by Bill and his South African colleague Desmond Collier using the country's far more diffuse "critical outcomes" framework as the starting point. We're pointing it out because it also includes "ethos" elements. Translate that word into "core values." They included them because South Africa's original framework was rich in "character" elements and had a clear moral as well as technical intent—something you might want to use in your ELC's framework as well.

Assessing Your Options

We hope that you've been inspired and impressed by what you've read. The heartfelt commitment and depth of thinking of those who developed these frameworks comes shining through in every example. And the richness of their vision about what our young people could be, and what they feel energized to foster, resonates deeply within us. But we've pointed out that they vary in their construction and in their grounding, and that's where you need to make some decisions before proceeding to create your own framework.

First, the role performer words embody and convey the major intent of our framework, so we recommend that you derive them first in your process—either one at a time, or in pairs. Choosing pairs allows you to expand the range and depth of the intended life performance domain. And as you go back through these examples, you'll see how their creators rather adeptly connected different aspects of a general domain of performance together in the pairs they created. You should consider this possibility as well, but it's certainly not mandatory.

Second, the qualitative attribute adjectives clearly add character and depth to the role performer words. Some frameworks use single ones, but most use pairs. In these cases, each adjective relates directly to *both* role performer words (a rule you should follow) but in complementary ways (the other rule you should follow if you choose to use pairs), giving greater breadth and depth to the intended life performance. You'll soon discover that every word really counts in this process, and we're confident that you'll find yourselves in vigorous debates over the inclusion of one adjective or another. Let those debates happen, and stay open and flexible.

Third, perhaps the biggest decision you'll have to make is whether to derive a framework that: (1) broadly takes all of the spheres of living and future conditions into account, (2) addresses each sphere specifically and directly, or (3) focuses on the five wellsprings with the spheres and future conditions used as grounding. For example, the very first example was derived directly (sphere by sphere) from the framework of spheres we showed earlier in this chapter. The other three examples in the first set address the spheres more broadly. Either strategy works well. Your decision may depend on the breadth of the spheres framework you generated, and how compelling you find the five wellsprings.

Diverse Paradigm Perspectives

Before moving on to the more technical next steps in this process, we're offering a divergent view on all of the above. What if we'd interviewed a number of "prominent" figures and asked them to consider the key strategic question that underlies all of these frameworks. How do you think they'd answer it? What would they most want emphasized? Here are some possibilities that jump out at us. What do you think of these possibilities?

- **Bishop Blase Cupich, religious**. Focus on Christian values, preparation for college, and responsibility.

- **Jeff Foxworthy, blue collar**. Focus on basic skills, preparation for work, and traditional values.

- **Howard Gardner, talent development**. Focus on multiple intelligences, experiential learning, diverse learning environments.

- **E. D. Hirsch, core knowledge**. Focus on the academic disciplines, subject knowledge, intellectual development.

- **Bill Spady, empowered living**. Focus on consciousness, creativity, collaboration, competence, compassion, and inner potential.

- **Jack Welch, leadership**. Focus on organizational effectiveness, economics, and future prosperity.

- **Oprah Winfrey, human relations**. Focus on humanistic values, leadership, and effective communication.

- **WikiOutcomes, customized**. Focus on personal and parental preferences and expectations.

Any others you'd care to add?

"We've Only Just Begun"

Yes, this is exciting work, but for all the entities that derived these inspiring frameworks, this was only the first step in their outcome-deriving process. They immediately learned that bringing these role-performance labels to life requires that they answer the first of two critical and tough questions:

How would we know one if we saw one?

This isn't an attempt to be clever. It's critical. The frameworks above may be highly relevant, timely, and significant, but they're not "operational." That is, it isn't clear what the learners will actually demonstrate/do/show that embodies the qualities and role performances implied in the labels. And until you have defined that, you simply have a framework of . . . well . . . inspiring labels. An extensive, detailed example of how this works is provided in chapter 10 of Spady's *Beyond Counterfeit Reforms*. There he operationalizes the South African example we just highlighted. But here's the short version for now.

Pick a framework from those above that interests you and select one life-performance role out of that set as your test case. We've noticed that "self-directed learner" has appeared several times, but it's also been connected here and there to some other interesting qualities and performances. So we're going to use the fourth framework in the first set as our example, but add two critical words to it. Notice:

Self-directed, inquisitive LEARNERS and THINKERS, *who consistently . . .*

The "who consistently" implies that they will be *doing* things that convince you that they are, in fact, what their label says they are. In other words, it's your bridge to answering the critical "How would we know one if we saw one?" question. These "doing" things we call "essential performance components" (EPCs). These EPCs are the concrete statements that actually define what the outcome means in observable terms. So here's what you should consider as you answer this question.

First, you've got four different elements to work with here, plus their various interrelationships. You can keep it simple by asking yourself, "What would convince me that I'm really observing self-direction in action? And what would convince me that I'm really seeing inquisitiveness in action?" Do this for all four words and for their interrelationships; that is, self-directed learners, inquisitive learners, self-directed thinkers, and inquisitive thinkers.

Second, as you begin to come up with ideas, translate them into phrases that begin with a clear action verb. For example, those two qualities—being self-directed and inquisitive—clearly suggest to us that learners would "initiate, investigate, explore, and probe" a variety of issues, problems, projects, and endeavors. Moreover, these actions directly help them "expand, extend, and enrich" their understanding of things, so that they can "describe, explain, and illustrate" them for you in considerable depth when they're finished. By our count that's ten different action verbs and related concepts you could confidently draw on to make several clear and compelling EPCs for this particular outcome.

Third, when you've completed your set of EPCs that convince you that you'd be observing a self-directed, inquisitive learner and thinker in action, take just those EPCs (without the label) to someone else familiar with this process and ask them to put a label on what you've created. If their label is close to the label you're working with, you're on secure ground. If it's way off, then you've got more thinking and wordsmithing to do with the EPCs. This "validity check" is a critical step in creating a solid and workable outcomes framework.

Fourth, hooray! Once you've developed a sound set of EPCs for each of your role-performer outcomes, you have solid gold in your hands. Why? Because they can readily be translated into the criteria you need for assessing student performance on all your outcomes! At assessment time—which can be ongoing in a well-developed ELC—you'll be asking your learners to show that they can do the things stated in the EPCs, both consistently and at increasing levels of depth as they learn and mature. This, in turn, means that you're no longer trapped in the testing box, which falsely assumes that remembering and processing content is the same as being able to do a variety of complex, life-relevant things with it.

This step in the process enables you to answer a second critical design question that parallels the first:

How can we assess them and document their development?

Just remember, the EPCs show the way, so craft them with insight and care.

Fifth, our advice here is directed toward you, the lead learner and teacher in this process, since we surely don't expect you, or a cast of thousands, to do all this EPC work at outcome-deriving time. Once your larger group of participants has generated a framework that is bulletproof and they can logically explain and defend, the task of creating EPCs should be turned over to your ELC's crack team of thinkers and wordsmiths. As you can see, this is a challenging task, and it's best left to people with the experience and expertise to handle it. So when the going gets tough, remember that doing it well is the real pathway to shifting your instructional paradigm and preparing your learners for Empowermentland.

A Bold Example

To help you along, we've included an example taken from the final framework shown above. Just to expand your perspective, we chose it because it's written as what we call a "declarations statement" with the learners themselves taking ownership for the outcome and declaring their "vision" of themselves as committed exemplars of its EPCs.

We are versatile, productive PERFORMERS and IMPLEMENTERS, developing our competent implementation capabilities by consistently:

- Devoting time to acquiring, practicing, and refining the skills needed for carrying out performance tasks confidently, fluently, and reliably
- Gathering information on the employability and performance standards used in a range of career fields that interest us, and translating them into goals for our own learning and performance
- Using these standards to set high performance goals for ourselves, and working to accomplishing them within agreed-upon time constraints
- Designing a range of different projects and endeavors that enable us to develop, apply, and demonstrate these standards at increasing levels of challenge and complexity
- Assessing and documenting the quality of our performance in relation to these established standards, and demonstrating what we can do to meet or exceed them

Note how directly and powerfully this outcome addresses the "quality" issue that motivates so many of today's reform efforts, but how insightfully it moves beyond the limited and limiting paper-pencil notions of learner achievement and performance. And note as well how thoroughly it promotes the future-focused, learner-centered, life-performance essence of an ELC's transformational philosophy and rationale.

Coming Up: The Next Big Design Question

There's another critical question to ask that can only be answered after you've answered the previous two. And it's one we'll be picking up directly in the next two chapters:

How can this outcome best be learned?

The answer will be embodied in your ELC's empowering learning system—where the rubber really meets the road to the future.

IMPLEMENTING AN EMPOWERING LEARNING SYSTEM: PARADIGM CHANGE IN ACTION

The main thing is to *make* the main thing the main thing!

Your organization is perfectly designed to get the results that you are now getting.

There are two key ways of viewing this component of your empowering learning community. The first is expressed in figure 5.1 on the following page. It is one of five critical components of a well-designed, fully integrated, and harmoniously functioning ELC, and we've been continually reinforcing that understanding throughout this book.

The second is to view it as *the* critical component of your ELC, with all of the others serving as its foundations. Illustrating the difference simply requires a small shift in the location of the diagram's elements (see figure 5.3). That shift moves your empowering learning system into the center, with defining/supporting arrows coming into it from the other four components. The only component we have not yet addressed is your aligned support structure, which will come in chapter 7.

Because your learning system is so central to what your ELC really is and does, we are devoting two chapters to it. This chapter will focus on the big paradigm shifts that occur when you truly define/drive/operate a learning system from a non-educentric perspective, and it will provide criteria and examples for keeping you on track in doing so. Chapter 6 will focus on the major restructuring aspects of your learning system—something that public systems have been unable to do for over a century.

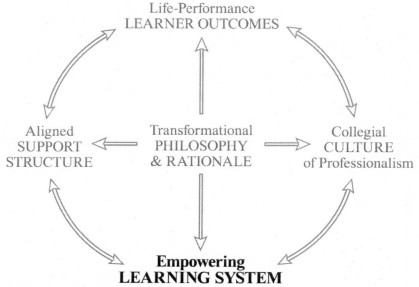

Life-Performance
LEARNER OUTCOMES

Aligned
SUPPORT
STRUCTURE

Transformational
PHILOSOPHY
& RATIONALE

Collegial
CULTURE
of Professionalism

**Empowering
LEARNING SYSTEM**

Figure 5.1.   Focusing on an ELC's learning system.

VISIONARY
Creative & Cutting Edge
Vision

SERVICE
Compassionate
& Dedicated
Support

AUTHENTIC
Conscious
& Ethical
Purpose

RELATIONAL
Collaborative
& Collegial
Ownership

QUALITY
Competent & Expert
Capacity

Figure 5.2.   The parallel emphasis of Total Leadership 2.0.

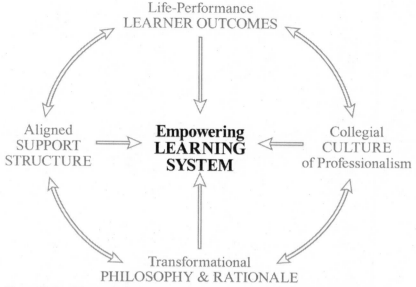

Figure 5.3. The central role of your empowering learning system.

But they now can, thanks to today's transformational technologies. In both cases we'll continually be referring to elements we've established in previous chapters because they all have a bearing on why, what, when, and where students learn.

The Big Picture Issues

From the middle of chapter 1 to this point in the book we have continually mentioned educentrism's fifteen boxes. Well, we're going to do it again, but differently this time. As we've grappled over the years with these boxes and looked for the linchpin that would unlock all of them, the best we've been able to do (without the benefit of your suggestions) is to narrow the challenge down to the interactions among three of them:

- **The Curriculum Subjects BⷭX**—because it defines and limits what learning and achievement are and provides the artificial content focus around which the system constructs requirements, grading and record keeping, accountability measures, and what are mistakenly treated as "outcomes."

- **The Time/Schedule B☐X**—because it has been the definer of everything the system has done over the past century—school years, semesters, grading periods, credit and reporting systems, attendance requirements, curriculum organization and access, eligibility conditions of all kinds, and faculty employment conditions.

- **The Grade Level B☐X**—because it defines the fixed opportunity and eligibility conditions in which the previous two boxes operate to create education's assembly line character—as if age were the one and only determiner of learning potential, readiness, rates, styles, and/or experience.

If you'll take a minute and consider how these three boxes interconnect and reinforce each other, you'll soon see that they're the bedrock/foundation of three major things: (1) how the other twelve boxes are defined and operate; (2) the impersonal, standardized, one-size-fits-all nature of our prevailing system; and (3) what today's educentric policy makers call "reform." We acknowledge that countless people can't imagine education not being organized and operated this way—which is why in chapter 1 we offered you one of many alternative "paradigm shifting" frameworks to consider, to use with your colleagues and constituents, and to advocate. Here it is again, for you to use in direct support of what follows.

As we've done before, we're inviting you here to consider the empowering alternatives shown on the right side of this framework, but this time please assess them in light of the reading and work you just did in chapter 4. We think it's possible to loosen the death grip of the three boxes above and the severe limitations of the related elements on the left by implementing one "silver bullet" component in your ELC—your framework of life-performance learner outcomes. But stay calm . . . it all depends on how you defined them.

Basing Your Learning System on Your Outcomes

When learner outcomes are about human beings (we hope yours are), they're no longer grounded in the curriculum subjects box, the time/schedule box, or the grade level box. When learner outcomes embody life-role performance abilities that reside within the spheres of living (again,

From a Limiting Reformer Orientation/Educentric Paradigm	To an Expansive Transformer Orientation/Empowerment Paradigm
In-the-box viewpoint	Outside-the-box viewpoint
Content-focused learning	Inner-focused learning
Disciplinary curriculum	Trans-disciplinary curriculum
Rational/logical thinking	Divergent/lateral thinking
Teacher-initiated/classroom-based learning	Learner-initiated/life experience learning
Graded structure and learning opportunities	Nongraded structure and learning opportunities
Academic achievement and advancement	Personal development and maturity
Transmission of accepted knowledge and understandings	Exploration of unique insights and possibilities
External expectations, control, and rewards	Internal motivation, control, and fulfillment
Premium on IQ learning	Focus on EQ development
Competitive organizational ethic	Collaborative organizational ethic
Quantitative measures of success	Qualitative measures of development
Closed-system thinking and operations	Open-system thinking and operations
Scheduled learning opportunities	Flexible learning opportunities
Getting right answers	Asking deeper questions
Adults as control and evaluation agents	Adults as learning and performance role models

we hope yours do), they're no longer grounded in those three boxes either. And when learner outcomes are about complex role performance abilities that take years to develop and mature (which follows from the previous two), they fully transcend these three boxes—which is another way of saying that the boxes are simply no longer relevant to the task at hand.

So if you really want to know what makes an ELC an ELC, it's the quote from Labovitz and Rosansky that appears at the beginning of this chapter:

The main thing is to make the main thing the main thing!

And in this case that main thing is your organizational purpose, expressed operationally in your framework of life-performance outcomes! If your framework isn't your ELC's main thing—the total focus of your instructional efforts and the reason your people come to work in the morning—don't expect anything of significance to change. The inertia embodied in the three boxes will exert its enormous influence, and you'll soon be back implementing and reinforcing all the things on the left side of this paradigm framework, simply because you lack the vehicle to shift to the empowerment side.

So for just a moment we're going to return to the heart of our work from two decades ago and emphasize the concept of being "outcome based." We've already explained the essence of outcomes in chapters 3 and 4, and we don't need to repeat it here. But we are going to zero in on the importance and power of the word "based"—because it's what's going to make your life-performance outcomes the heart and soul of your learning system and shift your ELC's operating paradigm. As we explained to countless audiences over a two-decade period, the term "outcome-based" means a combination of the six things described in the following box:

The term "outcome-based" means:

- **Defined by** your life-performance learner outcomes
- **Derived from** your life-performance learner outcomes
- **Aligned with** your life-performance learner outcomes
- **Focused on** your life-performance learner outcomes
- **Designed and organized around** your life-performance learner outcomes
- **Assessed against** your life-performance learner outcomes

---

Now just add these six different meanings up, multiply by ten, and take a look at the deep, serious "marching orders" you've given your ELC if you really want to shift it away from the industrial age, educentric paradigm.

To us the word "based" transforms outcomes themselves—from being "goals we hope we attain" to "the rock-solid foundation from which everything instructional emanates." This means that your assessments and record-keeping system are going to be "defined by, derived from . . . and assessed against" your framework of life-performance outcomes. And the same goes for your curriculum and your instructional approaches. Yes, "everything instructional" is going to be "defined by, derived from . . . and assessed against" your framework of life-performance outcomes. If this sounds impossible, it's not. Here are a couple of examples that show the way.

Ways of Basing Your Learning System on Your Outcomes

We've been told countless times by countless educators across the globe that being "outcome-based" is little more than exercising basic logic and common sense. If you want someone to learn something important, then clearly define what it is, explain and demonstrate it to them at the outset, assist them in various ways to learn and demonstrate it themselves, and validate that they have done so when they can do it really well and consistently. Certainly these simple steps get more complex as the nature of the outcome increases, but one fundamental remains constant:

The outcome is the reason for, and the focus of, everything in the process . . .

and in this case the outcome is a complex set of qualities and abilities expressed in "role performance" language—real people embodying highly significant empowering things that really matter in life.

The HeartLight South Africa Model

So to illustrate what this means operationally, let's consider for a moment the final outcomes framework presented in chapter 4. It's from an innovative alternative high school in Port Elizabeth, South Africa, and it was derived as an expression of the five wellsprings: living and learning consciously, creatively, collaboratively, competently, and compassionately in the world. One thing that makes this framework unique is that it is expressed as a set of "declarations" in which the HeartLight learners took direct ownership—that is, "We are . . .

> Aware, reflective SPIRITUAL BEINGS, continuously developing our conscious identity and inner growth

> Visionary, resourceful EXPLORERS and INNOVATORS, continuously developing our creative imaginations to the fullest

> Supportive, trustworthy TEAM PLAYERS and MENTORS, continuously developing our collaborative interactions with others

> Versatile, productive PERFORMERS and IMPLEMENTERS, continuously developing our competent implementation abilities

> Active, global CONTRIBUTORS and STEWARDS, continuously developing our compassionate involvement with the world

Notice how empowering this wording alternative is. The learners themselves are declaring their vision of themselves, both currently and in the future. This helped enormously in making these outcomes the focus/base of everything else they did.

But that still left the staff and learners at this ELC with a key question that really solidified these outcomes as the grounding of everything that would proceed instructionally:

> **What kind of learning experiences will our learners consistently require that directly foster these five life-performance outcomes?**

Note that "learning experiences" was their way of saying both "curriculum" and "instruction," and their answer took the form of a "program structure" that emphasized the content, contexts, and kinds of learning processes that would consistently and directly foster these five intended outcomes. So . . . to stimulate your thinking, here are their five key program areas, presented in the same order as above because each was explicitly designed to foster a specific outcome:

- **Personal Well-Being**—integrates many different kinds of holistic learning experiences, including spiritual development, meditation, nutrition, and all aspects of physical and psychological health, personal interests and talent development, mind-body integration, and any other individual interests in related areas. These experiences consistently strengthen the conscious identity of each learner as a unique being with incredible potential for enhancing the quality of life on the planet.

- **Creative Entrepreneurship**—integrates and applies many different kinds of theoretical and hands-on experiences related to all aspects of starting and operating a profitable small business. Its ongoing activities expand and apply each learner's creative imagination and problem-solving skills to the fullest as it emphasizes looking beyond the boxes, moving out of one's comfort zone, seeing possibilities when there appear to be no options, and daring to express their creative passion, even when it isn't in vogue.

- **Communication and Teamwork**—integrates and applies all aspects of interpersonal/interactive/collegial/relational activity with the broad range of communication, participation, connection, cooperation, collaboration, and belonging dimensions of human experience. Its focus on collaborative interaction encompasses the intent, emotion, and support embodied in sending and receiving information through words, symbols, touch, e-mails, music, videos, and movement.

- **Career Competence**—represents and supports the tangible, physical, technical, "know how—can do" side of life that gives expression to one's life purpose, interests, and passions. It emphasizes competent implementation by encouraging the purposeful exploration, development, integration, and application of a host of practical, technical, strategic, and role performance skills required of individuals in both basic and advanced levels of many career fields. This is done through direct instruction, job shadowing, collaborative hands-on project work, and mentoring relationships with career professionals in these fields.

- **Environmental Sustainability**—develops compassionate involvement in the world by fostering a deep awareness of (1) the complex array of conditions that affect the health and sustainability of both local communities and the global environment; and (2) the practical skills and tools to address those conditions constructively through individual and community-based service projects that focus on "adding value" to life beyond themselves— whether it be a friend, a member of the community, a stranger, or creatures in our natural environment.

While these five program areas depart significantly from the academic content structures with which we're all so familiar, they clearly embrace and utilize significant aspects of that content while addressing and using it in far more integrated and applied ways. Hence, we believe their future-focused, learner-centered, "functional" approach to learning and living resourcefully, productively, and harmoniously deserves attention and serious discussion as a template for ELCs everywhere.

Moreover, shortly after opening its doors in January 2003, the HeartLight Learning Community developed an assessment and reporting system for its students that was directly aligned with each of its life-performance outcomes. This system allowed for both staff and student input, and encouraged a dialogue around all of its key elements—certainly a radical departure from staff-controlled conventional letter grading and report cards.

The "Educating for Human Greatness" Model

While not as explicitly outcome-based as the HeartLight model, we'd like you to consider a second empowering example that emerged out of a close connection between the staff of a Utah elementary school and its constituents. It's the Educating for Human Greatness (EHG) model developed many years ago by Lynn Stoddard, the now-retired principal of the school, and his colleagues.

The model emerged in response to extensive parental input that there were more important educational priorities for their children than achievement in reading, writing, and arithmetic. These non-educentric priorities centered on (1) respect for each child's uniqueness, talents, and needs; (2) increased curiosity and passion for learning; and (3) improved interpersonal, communication, and collaboration skills. (Please pass this information from thousands of parents on to every educentrist that you know.) Out of the extensive discussions around this input emerged the school's overarching organizational purpose:

Develop great human beings to be contributors (not burdens) to society.

To realize this bold purpose, the entire community advocated a shift in priorities, and the traditional three Rs got redefined—from "goals" and ends in themselves, to "tools" that could help students grow in what came to be called the "seven dimensions of greatness." These seven dimensions became the equivalent of what we call life-performance outcomes, and they simultaneously served as the school's curriculum focus and structure. They are

1. **Identity**. Helping students learn who they are: individuals with unlimited potential; developing their unique talents and gifts to realize self-worth and a strong desire to be contributors to family, school, and community; and nurturing their health and physical fitness.

2. **Inquiry**. Stimulating curiosity; awakening a sense of wonder and appreciation for nature and humankind; and helping students develop the power to ask important, penetrating questions.

3. **Interaction**. Promoting courtesy, caring, communication, and cooperation.

4. **Initiative**. Fostering self-directed learning, will power, and self-evaluation.

5. **Imagination**. Nurturing creativity and creative expression.

6. **Intuition**. Helping students learn how to feel and recognize truth with their hearts as well as with their minds—developing spirituality and humility.

7. **Integrity**. Developing honesty, character, morality, and responsibility for self.

The school developed an extensive guide to the EHG model and its application. It provides more elaborate explanations of (1) each of the seven dimensions, (2) the nature of the learning experiences that foster them, and (3) tools for assessing both student progress and school effectiveness on each dimension.

The Operating Principles That Make "Based" Happen

If you're willing to return with us one more time to our outcome-based work of two decades ago, it will be easy to explain the two operating principles that really make the powerful word "based" work. The first of these we call the "clarity of focus on your culminating outcomes" principle. By that we mean that your curriculum, your instructional priorities and processes, your assessment and reporting system, and your motivations and expectations for learner success all must be openly, visibly, and clearly focused on and aligned with your "ultimate" outcomes. This principle has become completely familiar to most public educators today, but there's a huge difference: We're focused on life-performance outcomes, but most of them are politically forced to focus on educentric test scores.

The second principle is a bit more tricky and can be applied in two different ways. We call it the "design down from where you want to end up" principle. This means one of two related things:

1. Systematically design learning experiences "back" from their culminating point by continually asking, "What are they going to need to know and do in order to do *this* successfully?" Then after you have determined those prerequisites, ask this question again and again about each set of answers you get, working your way back to a set of true starting points. This process is known widely as "backward mapping," and it helps determine what is truly essential, where best to start, and the alternative routes for getting to the end point you desire.

    An observation we picked up years ago applies perfectly here: Mountain climbers always plan their climb from the peak back, because there may be only one way to take those last five steps.

2. Systematically bringing your culminating outcomes directly down intact into a learning experience and addressing them comprehensively there, but at a level of difficulty/complexity/maturity that matches the developmental level of the learners you're working with. For example, being visionary, resourceful explorers and innovators can be developed and enriched from the earliest days of primary school on through the last days of high school without missing a beat, simply because that life-performance outcome is "what we're here to develop and be every day of our educational experience." For short, we call this the "bring down" aspect of the "design down" principle.

So please take a moment and return to what we said a few pages back about the six meanings of "based." Look at each of them again in light of what we've just said about the "clarity of focus" and "design down" principles. From our perspective, these two principles definitely cover all six "bases" (so to speak)—which will delight Labovitz and Rosansky because you now know how *to make the main thing the main thing*. Hooray!

How Will We Know We Have One . . . an ELS, That Is?

We've given you tons of things to consider in designing and implementing your ELC and its empowering learning system, so we're going to do some bottom-line summarizing here that pulls many of these key elements together. In doing so, we'll be making only two assumptions. They're big ones, but there are only two of them.

Our first assumption is that you will be "viewing and doing" education from the transformer/empowerment side of the paradigm framework shown near the beginning of this chapter. (We want you to send us an affidavit confirming that.) If you do so, you'll be on the right path and the items below will reflect its spirit.

Our second assumption is that you'll be basing "everything instructional" on a future-focused, compelling life-performance outcomes framework. (We want you to send us a copy of the framework to confirm this.) If you do so, you'll naturally be doing everything on the right side of the paradigm framework, which will make your ELC's grounding bulletproof.

So if we paid a friendly visit to your ELC to see how you're implementation is coming along, we'd be particularly careful to note things being

- **Learner Centered**. Your teachers would be affirming and directly enhancing the natural curiosity, interests, talents, and sense of adventure in all your learners—and their colleagues as well.

- **Creative and Relevant**. Your teachers would consistently be encouraging their learners to explore and express all options open to them as they face tangible life issues—and there'd be tons of engagement around that.

- **Engaging and Experiential**. Your learners would be so engaged in self-directed, self-generated, self-assessing, and self-renewing real-life learning and living projects that it might take a while to identify the teacher.

- **Principled and Harmonious**. Everyone, old and young, would be demonstrating remarkable levels of consideration, collaboration, and emotional balance as they participate together and support each other's well-being and growth.

- **Community Based**. Your teachers and staff would be working closely with parents and community to plan, staff, and implement programs and use facilities that directly benefit both your learners and the community.

- **Empowering and Supportive**. All teachers, staff, and outside facilitators would consistently be encouraging all your learners to progress as far as their interests and capabilities will take them at any given time in any area of learning—and directly assisting them in doing so. (No boxes!)

- **Environmentally Sustainable**. Your programs and staff would consistently be advocating and implementing concepts, models, and strategies that honor and maximize the prudent use and conservation of the earth's natural resources.

- **Technologically Savvy**. Your staff would be consistently using advanced technologies to facilitate and customize the learning experiences of every student every day in all areas of learning. (No assembly-line instruction!)

Wow, if we could see all of that, we'd be the first to send a report to your state superintendent and board of education recommending that your entire staff be given gold-plated "Total Professional of the Decade" plaques and be invited to conduct leadership and change seminars all over your state. But to do that you're going to have to have the people who can pull all this off, and on that front we'd like to pass along some research from two distinguished colleagues, Renate and Geoffrey Caine.

Teaching for Empowerment

It takes an empowered person to empower others, and it takes an empowered thinker to be an empowered person. Moreover, it takes an empowered "perceiver" to be an empowered thinker and person. This is the core learning we've drawn from the Caines's world-renowned work on models of learning and teaching. But in this case the excitement is in the details, and we want to share some of the most important ones with you.

A Continuum of Approaches

From the Caines's perspective, what we've been describing throughout this book as in-the-box educentrism parallels what they describe as the top-down delivery model of traditional teaching known as direct instruction. They contrast it with the experiential, constructivist model that has gained considerable currency in the past decade, which they call learner-centered teaching. It, in turn, parallels what we've been calling the empowerment approach.

They've concluded that there is a continuum of instructional tools and approaches stretched between these two poles, and the farther teachers move toward the learner-centered pole the more of all the other approaches they can incorporate into their instructional repertory, including direct instruction. But this "cumulative" effect (our term for it) doesn't work in the other direction.

For example, "big-picture" thinkers and implementers can make good use of all the little and medium-sized pieces as they design or create something, but "little pieces" thinkers don't know what to do with the bigger, more theoretical, more expansive pieces. So they just keep on linking the little pieces together as if creating a chain—one chapter, or detail, at a time in the textbook (if we're allowed to mix metaphors).

After many years of research the Caines have concluded that many people cannot implement, and do not value, learner-centered teaching—and, therefore, cannot lead or help teachers use it—because they literally cannot "see"/envision how it works. For the Caines it comes down to the interplay between instruction and the perceptual orientations (i.e., paradigm thinking) that govern how one views and reflects on instruction, one's job role, appropriate learning environments, and the nature of reality itself. The bigger and wider one's perceptual field the better—which is exactly why we've devoted so much space in this book to expanding the perceptual field/map/paradigm about education as widely as we can: to enable you to approach your work from the biggest "big-picture"/transformational perspective possible.

Along the way the Caines draw a strong parallel between John Miller's (1993) three "positions" or "orientations to curriculum" and their own perceptual orientations to teaching and learning. Miller calls his three positions transmission, transaction, and transformation. "Transmission" is what teachers do when they conceive of the universe in "small reducible units" (direct instruction); "transactions" are what they engage in when the universe is seen as rational and intelligible and the (traditional) scientific method of cause and effect prevails (the Caines's Perceptual Orientation Twos); and "transformation" follows when the universe is seen as an interconnected whole (the Caines's Perceptual Orientation Threes).

Four Dimensions of Empowered Perception

There are four qualities or dimensions that serve as core elements of the Caines's perceptual orientations approach, and we're highlighting them here because they're critical to your selecting, developing, and appropriately using personnel who can fully support your ELC's empower-ment vision—a point we'll return to in chapter 7. They are

1. **From "power over others" to "self-efficacy grounded in authenticity."** You want Perceptual Orientation Threes on your team. They have moved from seeing power as primarily invested in others or outside forces to having a sense of self-efficacy where power and decision making reside predomi-nately within themselves. Accordingly, they are comfortable with empowering students, because students must be ad-equately empowered to make authentic and significant choices and decisions for your ELS to succeed.

2. **Expanded Cognitive Horizons**. Perceptual Orientation Threes have a big-picture grasp of things that makes it pos-sible for them to deal with content at very high levels. They understand the differences between facts, concepts, and the different levels of meaning, and they tend to be expert in at least one discipline or domain. They also have a "felt meaning" for other disciplines and for the ways in which subjects and disciplines interpenetrate each other. Finally, they have a sense of wholeness and interconnectedness, which enables them to see more connections among and between subjects, disciplines, and life. When you find them, hire and keep them.

3. **Self-Reference and Process**. Perceptual Orientation Threes have a significant capacity to self-reflect; they understand mind-fulness and have reflective intelligence. They see themselves as true lifelong learners. Moreover, they don't see themselves as needing to have the right answer but are adept at knowing how to turn the question around so that students see finding answers as their responsibility. Above all, they see themselves as constantly and necessarily learning—they are awake to each moment and, in the Caines's terms, "at home with the edge of possibility." They're the role models you want in your ELC.

4. **From "control" to "building relationships that facilitate self-organization."** Perceptual Orientation Threes' approach

to control has shifted dramatically. Much traditional direct instruction calls for a great deal of control over student behavior. Some of that control must be relinquished for genuine learner-centered teaching to occur. Perceptual Orientation Threes understand the relationships between information and experience, between learning and context, between students and teacher—which is why they can facilitate self-organization within the classroom and the ELC. Discipline is a secondary concern because it is a natural consequence of learning organized around meaningful projects and activities. Student responsibility lies everywhere—from keeping classrooms and your ELC orderly, to helping others evaluate their work and challenging each other. If you want your ELC to be "principled and harmonious," hire Threes.

In addition, we've shared our five wellsprings with the Caines as important elements in learner-centered teaching, and they're in full agreement that moving from orientation one to orientation three clearly involves expanding one's consciousness, creativity, collaboration, competence, and compassion.

They also strongly agree with us that educational leaders need a vision, and one aspect of that vision should include a grasp of what great teaching looks like, and a way to get there. Leaders need to be able to see great teaching in operation and have a good understanding of how approaches one, two, and three differ. With these distinctions clearly in mind, leaders are better positioned to see the deep interconnectedness of issues like attendance, discipline, community, student engagement, and academic results, and to make good decisions about teacher selection and programs of professional development.

The Action Learning Model

If we were to go back and review all of the life-performance learner outcomes frameworks in chapter 4, we'd find remarkable similarities among them, even though they use different words to define the kind of learner, thinker, innovator, collaborator, producer, and/or contributor they envision. As you might expect, everywhere we worked teachers expressed considerable concern about how they were going to directly facilitate the range of role performance learning that their particular outcomes framework required.

We agreed with them and began to look for a set of strategies and processes they could use that would help all of them manage and facilitate student learning in a comprehensive and effective way. Out of these deliberations emerged a few versions of what came to be called the action learning model—"action" because this was all about the learners actively engaging in their own development. You'll find one of the most widely used versions described in chapter 11 of Spady's *Beyond Counterfeit Reforms* (2001). Regardless of the details, these variations all shared four key things:

1. **Elements of teaming, collaborative work, and interpersonal communication**. Learners often work in learning teams on significant, larger-scale projects and must learn and apply a range of collaborative and communication skills.

2. **Learner-initiated exploration and reflective analysis on what is discovered**. Learners actively explore things of interest and significance and learn to analyze what they are encountering and "make meaning" from it.

3. **Translating that learning into a tangible product or demonstration**. Learners become implementers, performers, demonstrators, and producers of what they learn, regularly exhibiting it openly in a variety of ways.

4. **Critically self-assessing and documenting its quality**. Learners become "quality control" managers of their own work and routinely learn to self-assess its merits at every stage of their "discovery to demonstration" process.

Teachers soon discovered that, by consistently implementing these four action learning processes as a regular way of providing instructional support, they could address and facilitate almost all of the elements in their district's or school's life-performance outcomes framework all the time.

Clearly these action learning processes move teachers and instruction miles beyond the limited and limiting constraints of direct instruction without abandoning it when appropriate. And they directly encourage and support all learners in expressing and enhancing their unique talents, interests, and attributes. Moreover, they directly honor and advance learners' capacities for self-directed, self-assessing, self-governing, and self-renewing learning and living—what we believe to be the ultimate embodiment and expression of empowerment.

We obviously encourage you to consider using this or similar models in your ELC because they constitute powerful approaches to developing learners' intellectual, intuitive, interpersonal, emotional, and applied performance capabilities. And since it encourages them to continuously and critically assess the relevance and significance of everything they experience, a well-conceived model such as this is key to your ability to achieve a dynamic balance between

- Focus and flexibility

- Purpose and freedom

- Challenge and support

- "Partial" and "whole-brain" learning

- Individual engagement and team endeavor

- Inner growth and applied competence

- Individual success and the common good

That's a lot to say for an instructional approach that embodies the substance and spirit of what it means to implement a genuinely empowering learning system.

USING MASS CUSTOMIZED LEARNING TO RESTRUCTURE FOR SUCCESS

Your organization is perfectly structured to get the results that you are now getting.

Leaving the past is central to progress. The very nature of an executive's job is to make decisions about committing resources to the possibilities of tomorrow. . . . Effective leaders know that a decision is not complete until it is put into action.

—Peter Drucker

The fifteen educentric boxes that we've been discussing throughout this book will be broken and strewn all over the assembly-line floor. Hooray!

There's a time-honored premise in organizational theory: "Form follows function." From our perspective this means that "Your organization's structures are the result of the processes you're employing." Structures are consistently recurring patterns—school starts at 8:00 each morning, no matter what—and those patterns, and the boundaries that define them, strongly affect what happens, when, and where.

So, while we hate to argue with all the great theorists of our age, we think today's educational system is just the opposite: Structure constrains and limits process! Said differently, the prevailing structures/patterns/boxes that define and characterize our educational system seriously limit what people can do, who does it, how they do it, and when it's done—unless, of course, individuals really want to stick their necks out, buck the

Life-Performance
LEARNER OUTCOMES
Aligned
SUPPORT
STRUCTURE
Empowering
LEARNING
SYSTEM
Collegial
CULTURE
of Professionalism
Transformational
PHILOSOPHY & RATIONALE

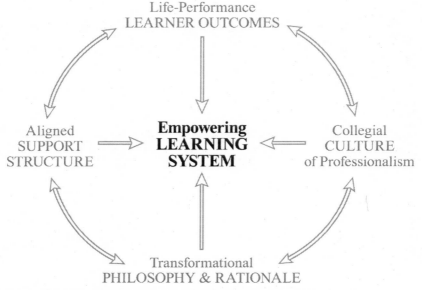

Figure 6.1. The central role of empowering learning systems.

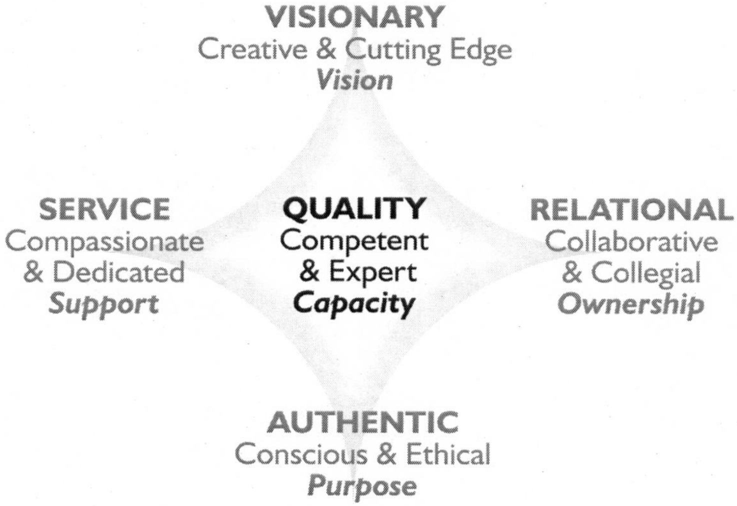

VISIONARY
Creative & Cutting Edge
Vision
SERVICE
Compassionate
& Dedicated
Support
QUALITY
Competent
& Expert
Capacity
RELATIONAL
Collaborative
& Collegial
Ownership
AUTHENTIC
Conscious & Ethical
Purpose

Figure 6.2. The parallel emphasis of Total Leadership 2.0.

tide, swim upstream, test the system's limits, and risk serious negative consequences for their efforts.

So we're going to shift our focus in this chapter from the case we've been building throughout this book concerning *why* we need to refocus and redefine education and *what* that refocusing and redefining is all about, to *how* that refocusing and redefining can proceed "on the ground." In other words, we're going to show how real restructuring can happen using today's transformational technologies as the key driver of change.

Think Silver Lever, Not Silver Bullet

But let's be clear at the outset. We're not talking about technology as the "silver bullet" that's going to magically transform educentric, industrial age schools into empowerment age ELCs—we've already devoted five chapters to explaining what has to be put in place if that's really going to happen. Nor is this simply about creating cyberschools—give every learner a computer, let them explore the universe of knowledge with it, and the problem is solved—although that might end up being a part of the total picture. (By the way, there are several influential books available on that subject already.)

Instead, our focus here is on how ELCs can use today's amazing technological tools to, once and for all, abandon/replace the assembly-line structures and functions that plague our system with something that we call "mass customized learning" (MCL). So rather than thinking of technology as a silver bullet that can't possibly foster all of the life-performance outcomes that will be in your ELC's framework, consider it instead as a "silver lever" that has the potential to release the stranglehold that the fifteen boxes have on learners, learning, and learning systems. When you and your colleagues pull that lever, no longer will schooling be a case of . . .

> Specific students of a specific age must learn specific things on a specific schedule in a specific classroom from a specific teacher using specific materials and methods so that they can pass specific tests on specific dates—and only then will they specifically be called "OK."

Moreover, the fifteen boxes that we've been discussing throughout this book will be strewn all over the assembly-line floor. Hooray!

The Essence of Mass Customized Learning

The term mass customization comes from the very modern world of business. We reference it numerous times in chapters 1 and 3 of *Total Leaders 2.0*, and we believe that those of us in twenty-first-century North America actually take it for granted, even though we don't know it by that name. It's what businesses are able to do on a very large scale to meet the individual needs of clients in a timely and very efficient way. In fact, they're so used to it at Starbucks that if you just order a "small coffee," the staff will ask again to be sure they didn't miss something you said.

For example, here's a real experience that happens hundreds of thousands of times per day, seemingly without a hitch. (Please know that this is not an embedded commercial for Apple Inc. for which we receive royalties. Oh, we wish!) We choose it because it illustrates the essence of technology's current capacity to almost instantaneously customize services for both the client and the service provider. So please consider that Apple's iStore:

- Allows you to select and buy your favorite individual songs

- For only 99 cents each—cheaper than in '79

- Immediately downloads them to your computer or iPod, and you're listening to Anne Murray sing "You Needed Me" within minutes

- Within seconds your VISA is debited

- Anne Murray's bank account is credited

- All totally "friction free"

- No one touched anything

- No one had to do any work

- And Steve Jobs buys another expensive bottle of merlot!

Now that we've got your attention, please read each of these bullets again slowly and give yourself some time to reflect on the actual experience. Had we suggested this fifteen years ago, your response would have been *"No way!"* But today, we estimate that well over 50 percent of our readers have actually had this experience.

Do you see any possible application to education? We sure do, and it's a great example of what we call "cross-industry transfer," which means exactly what it says. Industries in one area can borrow, adapt, and apply ideas and technologies from another field and benefit enormously from their use. To further reinforce our notion of mass customization, just consider how education could benefit from these cross-industry examples by learning from

- **Sylvan Learning** about meeting individual learner needs, high expectations, and accountability for learning

- **Wells Fargo** about being open for business 24/7

- **Michael Dell** about how to meet the individual needs of millions of clients at low cost—with an amazing record-keeping system

- **Wal-Mart** about how to use bar codes to organize, manage, and communicate everything important about a product or their business

- **Amazon.com** about profiling to meet the needs of individual clients

- **Verizon** about complex record keeping and making information available to those with "a need to know"

- **iTunes** about how to simultaneously act on the listening/entertainment preferences of millions of individual customers

- **Apple Inc.** about how to put 20,000 songs, plus a movie or two, and all your photo albums on a gadget small enough to put in your shirt pocket

- **3M** about risk taking, innovation, and learning from failures

- **The University of Phoenix** about preparing and credentialing people with limited time to devote to their studies

- **Microsoft** about their calendar for scheduling meetings

- **Google** about finding any information that you desire . . . usually with only two clicks

- **Wikipedia** about how to harness the power of volunteers

A Cross-Industry Possibility

So surely the transformational technologies that have enabled these industries to develop and implement such amazing capabilities can equip Willow Creek iSchool—a public primary school—to allow Lincoln, one of its "third graders," to:

- Download learning objective 3.2.4, dividing with two numbers in the dividend

- Review his completed objectives, electronic portfolio, and his next challenges

- Select his learning style and content interest area related to objective 3.2.4 and, within sixty seconds, begin working on that activity

- Demonstrate his competence when completed about forty-five minutes later

- Have his electronic performance portfolio immediately updated and record "Accomplished" for learning objective 3.2.4

- Watch a short film clip of Peyton Manning throwing three touchdown passes in the 2007 Super Bowl as a reward for completing the objective, and . . .

- Have his parents and Willow Creek learning coach Mary Brown notified by auto e-mail of his success, and drop him a personalized e-mail "attaboy" for it

And notice, just like Apple's iStore:

- All of this was totally "friction free"

- Lincoln's learning coach didn't have to touch anything

- No one but Lincoln had to do any work

- And Lincoln's mom calls his grandpa to boast about Lincoln's intelligence, his cuteness, and their plans for that Dartmouth application!

So while some educators may balk at the label "mass customized" because it sounds so "business-like," mechanical, and/or impersonal, the proof is in the pudding, not the label on the box. MCL is indeed a new vision for instructional delivery, and we've had a number of thoughtful and lively discussions regarding what to call this learner-responsive vision. In the end, we chose to stick with MCL because the label is descriptive of what our vision will do for learners and for an ELC. Moreover, the label is "sticky"; it's easy to remember, and it clearly supposes that it's time for educators to embrace "cross-industry transfer" and learning. Don't let the label stop you from giving your total support to a concept and process that has the potential to transform education.

But words *do* make a difference to people, so if you prefer the name personalized learning, or even comprehensive personalized learning (CPL)—which are warmer and fuzzier—that's just fine. Change the label for your staff and community if you wish, but embrace the learner-centered vision behind it. Or, when your eyes read MCL, just tell your brain those letters are really CPL and keep on focusing on the larger issue: a significant alternative to industrial age assembly-line instruction and learning opportunities. The result, as promised at the beginning of the chapter, is that

The fifteen educentric boxes that we've been discussing throughout this book will be broken and strewn all over the assembly-line floor. Hooray!

And the two most broken and strewn ones among them will be ❑ The Time/Schedule B❑X and ❑ The Opportunity B❑X.

Education will no longer be time-defined and schedule-driven, and opportunities to learn and advance in a timely manner will expand enormously. Moreover, since we believe in "truth in advertising" and we're promoting both empowerment and customization in this book, we fully expect that you will take what follows, just as you did with all the examples of life-performance outcomes in chapter 4, and create your own best version of whatever our MCL vision and examples suggest. In short, anything you can do to break free from the assembly-line delivery of instruction and unlock yourself from its mechanistic constraints is a step in the right direction. Just be sure your vision is bold enough to get you past those first few steps.

MCL: A Vision for Expanding Learning Opportunities

Our vision for expanding learning opportunities is a bold one. It is not about helping a third-grade teacher individualize spelling or an English III teacher to motivate students by allowing them to choose from three literature classics. Our vision is about using transformational technologies to customizing learning for a high school of 2000, for an entire middle school, for all learners at all times in all locations, period. It's about meeting the individual learning needs of every learner every hour of every day. There is nothing magic about it; the magic is already in the technologies.

But let's be very clear; we're not suggesting that transformational technologies (TTs) should, or could, take over education and learning. Rather, we believe they should be consistently applied whenever and wherever it's appropriate so that educators can do better as professionals what they've always wanted to do: empower their learners to thrive in a changing world. TTs are tools and enablers, not the message. They're resources and extenders, not the professional. How could TTs possibly replace professional learning facilitators in fostering the range and depth of life-performance outcomes described in chapters 4 and 5? And yes, we said "learning facilitators"! That's our outside-the-box way of thinking about and defining those who "teach" in an ELC.

Levels of Technology-Driven School Systems

1. Totally online. The learner determines the rate, the content, and the learning style.
2. Totally online. The system determines the learner outcomes, the rate, and the content.
3. A balance of online and teacher-facilitated learning, based upon best approaches to learning.
4. Classroom-based instruction with opportunities for online support.
5. Exclusively school/classroom-based instruction.

To provide an appropriate focus as we begin our vision trip, let's revisit our definition of an organizational vision:

**A concrete picture of what we will look like, feel like,
and be like when operating at our ideal best.**

And remember, to be powerful, visions must be bold, be inspirational, run well ahead of our present ability to do them, and provide hope for an ideal future. Our MCL vision clearly meets all of these criteria.

Weight-Bearing Walls: Our Vision's Strength

Our picture of an "ideal best" instructional delivery system (MCL) had its beginning several years ago when we were asked to work with Doug Parks and about seventy of his superintendent colleagues from Lake County, Illinois. The term "mass customization" was finding its way into the futures, change, and leadership literature at that time, and we were asked to explore with them if the technology that made it possible for businesses to deliver customized products and services might be transferable to education. In other words, might schools be able to mass customize learning? After our presentation and considerable discussion in small groups, they readily acknowledged that our present assembly-line learning system was outdated, ineffective, and in need of significant change, and they weren't defensive or offended when we compared education practices to business practices.

We had designed the seminar around the metaphor of weight-bearing walls (WBWs). Think of them as the walls of the key boxes that keep our industrial age system in place and make it nearly impossible to change. Our challenge was to show them how transformational technologies could replace all of those seemingly essential walls with new structural supports that would facilitate MCL and paradigm change. So we offered the following observations:

1. The roofs of buildings are held up by walls. Some are weight bearing, others are not. Construction managers must know the difference because . . .

2. If you remove a WBW, the roof will collapse, destroying the structure and probably causing severe injury to everyone involved.

Table 6.1.

Weight-Bearing Walls	What They Do for Us Now	What We Could Do If We Didn't Have Them
Grade levels	Allow us to group students and move them through the system	Continuous progress of individuals/everyone
Students assigned to classrooms	Allow us to divide/group students and assign staff	Bring students with similar needs together with a teacher
Class periods/bell schedule	Provide logistical control of staff and students	Put everyone in control of where they need to be
Courses/curriculum	Divide content in chunks to fit a course	Allow life-role learner outcomes to determine direction and progress
Textbooks	Provide content in chunks to fit the master schedule	Get content that fits learner needs from anywhere
Paper and pencil	Written records of student performance	Digital and flexible records of student performance
ABC grading system	Allow us to evaluate learners/students	Allow each student to create an electronic portfolio
Report cards	Communicate with parents re: student performance	Real-time communication re student learning via electronic portfolio
Learning happens in schools	Control, accountability, and administrative convenience	Learning in real-life contexts, use of community resources
Nine-month school year	Allows parents to schedule vacations and harvest crops (a little fun here)	Continuous learning and development; eliminate student learning regression

3. To safely remove a WBW, one must first replace it with another device that safely supports the roof and keeps them operating successfully.

4. Schools, like other organizations, also have operational WBWs that support their present purpose and patterns of functioning, which can safely be replaced with other supporting devices.

To support this profoundly important fourth point, we've created a WBW matrix that spells out many of our current "essential walls," the tangible supporting alternatives to them, the technologies that make the alternatives possible, and the entities that are already employing these technologies in a client-focused, mass-customized way.

Please take a long and hard look at the large matrix contained in table 6.1—not as a "how to" piece, but as a "Yes, I think that this is possible"

Today's Power Technology	Who Is Doing It Now
Mass customization of products and services	Apple iTunes, Google, Amazon.com, Bing
Complex schedule coordination	Yahoo Schedule, Microsoft, Google, iMac
Complex schedule coordination	Yahoo Schedule, Microsoft, Google, iMac
Any content available from anywhere at any time	Wikipedia, Bing, Google, the Web
Virtually all information is available on the Internet	Google, Bing, Wikipedia
Thumb drives that hold 8 gigs for $19.95	Best Buy, Wal-Mart, Dell, HP, Fry's Electronics
Home production of all types of media	YouTube, MySpace, Facebook
Digital communication, secure passwords, encryption	Banks, online retailers, eBay
Anyone can learn anything from any place at any time	eCyber schools, exchange programs, mentoring, shadowing
Business is conducted from anywhere 24/7/365	Virtually all online information sources and businesses

piece—because it underlies almost all of what follows. And as you do so, please consider the following important points about the alternative support structures we're suggesting:

- They're consistent with the most basic research regarding learning—the present WBWs are not.

- They're consistent with the intrinsic motivators of our youth—the present WBWs are not.

- They directly support learner empowerment, sometimes called "fostering self-directed, lifelong learners"—the present structure does not.

- They're all implementable and doable through relatively inexpensive business applications already in place.

Without question, the WBW matrix in table 6.1 offers an enormous amount to consider, but much of it is familiar. As we view it, the WBW elements described on the left are all a part of the institutionalized entity we know as "school," and the ELC/MCL alternatives offered for each appear to the right of them. This parallels the "from–to" paradigm-shifting framework we presented in chapters 1 and 5, and we encourage you to revisit it and, once again, note the significant difference in both substance and vocabulary there as well as here.

We continue to repeat this observation because the words you use are critical to establishing the mind-set and culture of expectations that will enable you and your people to embrace these MCL alternatives. And we want to point out here, if you haven't already noticed it, that we've been very careful to avoid using conventional educentric terminology throughout this book for this very reason. We want you to be thinking, talking, and enacting a different way of educating, and words/labels/terms are a critical part of that change.

When your people really get the hang of this—no doubt through constant monitoring and reinforcement on your part at the beginning—it will start to be fun. This is certainly the case with one of our client districts where there are many good-natured laughs as their conversations and e-mails are critiqued for "paradigmatically correct vocabulary." So please don't take this vocabulary issue lightly. It is a powerful tool for changing thinking and giving new meanings to your transformational change efforts.

Restructuring for Successful Learning

Let's assume for now that the WBW matrix that you've just examined has convinced you that proceeding with MCL is both desirable and feasible. Where do you start?

Our answer won't surprise you, but it's not offered casually: with your framework of life-performance outcomes and its "design down"/"bring down" principles, described in chapter 5. Why? For three key reasons: (1) they reflect your ultimate intentions for your learners, (2) they are the foundation on which new paradigm curriculum is based, and (3) there are lots of enabling skills and concepts that must be addressed and developed in order for learners to ultimately demonstrate them at high levels of complexity and mastery. That's why design down (build back from where you want to end up) and bring down (at levels of complexity suitable for a learner's developmental stage and maturity) are vital.

Moreover, the outcomes themselves vary enormously in terms of the kinds of knowledge and abilities they require. Some are far more interpersonal and interactive than others. They require lots of direct, face-to-face engagement with people and certainly can't be learned and practiced sitting in front of a computer or listening to teacher presentations. Neither can a variety of applied performance abilities such as music, art, drama, public speaking, athletics, public service, and building/crafting/growing tangible or living things. Those are huge areas of learning that cannot be appropriately and directly fostered through online or computer-based learning alone. They require "applied formats" of various kinds, not conventional classrooms or computer labs, and the time to really develop and hone the competences involved.

There are, of course, a host of other left brain cognitive and technical knowledge and skills that can efficiently and effectively be learned via computers on a schedule, and at a pace, that suits the individual learner. Since much of this involves fairly routine "content transmission," it's where computer-based learning can really pay off for you, leaving your professional staff more time to do those things that can't be done effectively via technology. In addition, a lot of this may involve developing what we call "tool skills" like reading and math—things that are building blocks of more complex outcomes (not the outcomes themselves) and for which a range of useful curriculum and content-accessing software now exists.

Consider that informal surveys we've conducted when working with groups indicate that both teachers and principals believe that at least half of what we are now asking students to learn could best be learned one-on-one with a computer. Some groups, usually from secondary schools, offer much higher estimates—as high as 75–80 percent. Hence, you can readily see where computer-based instruction could be an incredible time and personnel saver for your ELC under the right circumstances.

Two Key MCL Design Questions

Given all of the above, we believe that two critical design questions immediately arise for you and your colleagues as you consider moving forward on the MCL path. And we recommend that you have clear answers to both before launching anything:

1. How is this learner outcome best learned?

2. What kind of delivery formats will we make available to support this?

Your answers to the first question will, of course, directly influence how you answer the second. As a prompt to both, here's a basic list of learning modes/formats that an ELC might come up with which at least initially addresses both questions. For example, we're guessing that your assessment of these two questions will generate alternatives showing that particular outcomes or objectives can best be learned

1. By individuals alone, online, with facilitator support, or

2. In interactive seminars/endeavors/settings, or

3. Via large group presentations or reading, or

4. Via personally selected and directed projects, or

5. Through hands-on experience, shadowing, or apprenticeships

You may come up with other possibilities or describe these with different words, but either way, be absolutely clear about having a range of very different kinds of learning formats available if you really want MCL to work for you. You can explore a host of possibilities for organizing and scheduling formats like these in *Teaching the Digital Generation* by Kelly, McCain, and Jukes. And for real-life examples of alternative high schools implementing most of these learner-centered restructuring features, check out the great work being done by EdVisions Schools in Henderson, Minnesota (www.edvisionsschools.org).

Getting Ready for Rollout

"Ready for rollout" is a business term that applies here. Companies don't put something on the market until it is "ready for rollout," which means that you can't do it a little at a time. MCL is somewhat like that; it can't be properly "rolled out" before the infrastructure is in place to support it.

So, for example, if half or more of what our students truly need to master can be learned online or with a computer—which is exactly what our Willow Creek iSchool example early in the chapter was illustrating— your ELC's curriculum, instruction, and technology specialists will have to buy, borrow, or create computer-based learning opportunities for each of those objectives. While gearing up for this is a large up-front task for sure, many online instructional programs already exist, and other ELCs that are implementing MCL should be ready to offer assistance.

We recommend that you use the following items as a checklist to ensure that you're really ready to launch MCL successfully. We'll be describing and discussing these items in more detail shortly, so you can use this list as a guide as you continue. You'll know that you have MCL ready for rollout when you've replaced your fifteen educentric boxes with the following:

1. **Curriculum as Learner Outcomes.** Your learning experiences for students will all be written in "learner outcome" format, based on your framework of life-performance outcomes and the design down/bring down principles.

2. **Learner Outcomes Categorized as to Learning Format.** This is the answer to question 1: "How is this learner outcome best learned?"

3. **Computer-Based Learning for Many Outcomes/Objectives.** Whether online or in your ELC's system, these enabling outcomes (and their accompanying learning activities, assessments, record keeping, and reporting) can be accessed and accomplished by individual students 24/7/365.

4. **Learner Outcomes Requiring an Interactive, Seminar Format.** These are outcomes best learned in an interactive, high-engagement "seminar" format. Their prerequisites, learning facilitators, agendas, timeframes, and scheduled opportunities are regularly communicated to learners.

5. **Learner Outcomes Requiring Experiential Environments**. Some outcomes require major engagement outside of your ELC. Suitable arrangements must be made for them—facilitators, learning sites, and so forth.

6. **Scheduling Technology for Learners**. Electronic calendars to allow learners to create their personal learning schedules and help learning facilitators to plan, organize, advertise, and conduct the seminars they offer.

7. **Accountability Technology for ELC Leaders**. This tracking technology allows administrators to know the learning schedules and physical location of all learners at all times. It also provides electronic learning portfolios that track the academic progress of each learner, specific groups, and the total community of learners.

8. **Reporting Technology**. This technology allows those with "a need to know" to access individual learner outcome records, electronic portfolios, present learning activities, and projected future activities/schedules.

The Interactive Seminar Format

These "seminars" are vehicles for addressing many of your life-performance outcomes, and they offer opportunities for in-depth investigations, engagement, and interaction. Because they're so central to higher-level exploration and learning, they need to be carefully designed, staffed, and field tested. Depending on the outcome focus and topic, they could run from ten instructional hours in length to an entire year, but the latter would be an exception. Forty hours might well be the norm. Learners would schedule seminars online, be immediately informed if they were admitted, or when the next available one is scheduled should it already be filled.

One or more learning facilitators would design, schedule, and staff each one, and serve as a learning mentor to all who attend. They'd also determine the attendance cap and learning prerequisites for each seminar and offer it as often as learner demand required throughout the year. We expect them to become experts on a number of seminar topics and demonstrate what lifelong learning is all about in those areas. (Does that sound like "facilitators are real professionals" to you, too?)

If we took just one life-performance outcome from the HeartLight example we highlighted in chapter 5 and used it to generate significant seminar topics, just think of the stimulating and significant array of things you could generate from

Supportive, trustworthy TEAM PLAYERS and MENTORS, continuously developing our collaborative interactions with others—

and the variety of orientations and skills you could develop around interpersonal communication, team building, relationship dynamics, beliefs and values, consensus building, conflict resolution, group decision making, facilitating and mentoring, et cetera, et cetera. It's an incredible opportunity to step outside the standard curriculum box and engage young people fully in issues of real significance to them and the larger society.

The Experiential Environments Format

If any format really blows open the boundaries of what it means to establish and manage an empowering learning system, it's this one. And how germane it is to life-performance outcomes like

Visionary, resourceful EXPLORERS and INNOVATORS, continuously developing our creative imaginations to the fullest

Versatile, productive PERFORMERS and IMPLEMENTERS, continuously developing our competent implementation abilities

Active, global CONTRIBUTORS and STEWARDS, continuously developing our compassionate involvement with the world.

It certainly doesn't take much imagination to see that outcomes like these literally demand learning experiences that stretch all of the conventional academic content, competence, and classroom context boundaries that we're so accustomed to. And we'll be the first to suggest that both honoring and directly fostering the substance and spirit of outcomes like these will require, for starters, a dramatically expanded staff focus on building and coordinating community: connections, partnerships, mentoring and shadowing arrangements, learning environments, project settings, and assessment processes.

And we'll also acknowledge that the pivotal factor here is learner responsibility—which may be why some of the team building and relationship dynamics abilities addressed in the seminars might need to be established as prerequisites for off-site participation in these kinds of experiences. The potential for deeply enriching and empowering experiences resides in this format option, as does a great deal of "supervision risk."

New Professional Staff Roles

MCL encourages and requires educators to be, and act as, professionals. That is difficult to do in light of the self-contained/self-constrained nature of what we've shown as The Role/Control B☐X, containing the people called "teachers" who implement and manage the assembly-line delivery system we've characterized as follows:

> Specific students of a specific age must learn specific things on a specific schedule in a specific classroom from a specific teacher using specific materials and methods . . . et cetera.

People in this box are compelled to perform more like assembly-line workers than professionals, and MCL happily changes this role identity. That's why we think that "learning facilitator" is a more descriptive and a far better professional label than "teacher." In an MCL system, learning facilitators have a number of responsibilities, nearly all professional. They include

- Being the learning coach to twelve to fifteen learners

- Creating and delivering seminars that enable learners to accomplish complex life-performance outcomes

- Guiding and mentoring learner-initiated projects

- Teaming with other learning facilitators to continuously improve learning experiences and the overall quality and success of the ELC

As learning coaches, they will:

- Advise and mentor twelve to fifteen learners

- Examine learners' options and connect their learning experiences to their vision of the future

- Be the key communication link between the learners, their parents, and the ELC

- Analyze, assess, and evaluate individual learner progress

Note that by redefining the traditional role of "teacher"—especially at the high school level—MCL shifts the paradigm of instruction from a "stand and deliver" construct to a much more in-depth "guide on the side" orientation consistent with the Caines's work, described in chapter 5. Little time has to be spent delivering basic skills and content. Computers can handle a great deal of that. Consequently, human interaction and modeling are enhanced through the clarifying, assisting, probing, guiding, and encouraging that learning facilitators and coaches consistently do with learners.

Transforming Grading and Record Keeping the MCL Way

We're avoiding names here to protect the guilty—namely a very famous pioneer in the high tech world. In his first major book he happened to address the benefits that technology could bring to education. The essence of his utterly underwhelming recommendations was that computers could help teachers compute GPAs faster and more accurately!

Yes they can, if you want to stay entrenched in the industrial age Grading/Marking B☐X, the traditional Achievement B☐X, and the win-lose Ranking B☐X for another few decades. But in case you want to liberate yourself from those profoundly disempowering features of educentric education, we recommend that you expand your paradigm perspective beyond that of our famous high tech author. And we strongly recommend that you start by reading chapter 5 of Spady's *Beyond Counterfeit Reforms*. Its title is "Exposing the Numbers Game," and its message is direct and compelling. The essence of his argument is reflected in one of our favorite slides, shown in the shaded box below:

> If they give you this much space
> ⌐
> to record a student's learning,
> they sure must not want to know much!

And boy, does this slide create a stir!

The issue, pure and simple, is that grades, averages, GPAs, and rankings aren't the learning, or real achievement, at all. They're simply numerical codes that disguise and distort the real substance. They can't tell you what a student knows, can do, or has accomplished. They just provide a vague symbol that's supposed to represent the quality or accuracy of what was done. If you really want to know about their learning, you need totally different kinds of assessment, record keeping, and reporting tools—ones that document and contain the actual substance/evidence of learning and its products and impact on the world. And the key words for what that might be, and how it might look, are demonstrations, exhibitions, and portfolios. There are two kinds of the latter—tangible and electronic. MCL values both, but really capitalizes on the electronic.

Electronic Learning Portfolios

Letter grades and grade averages are inconsistent with learner outcomes and/or with any organization that values quality. Based on what we said in chapter 7 of *Total Leaders 2.0* about quality, we think you'd have a tough time justifying a B− in physics to W. Edwards Deming. (Yes, we know, he passed away in 1994, but we trust that you get the point.) Outcomes are tangible, criterion-defined demonstrations of learning. You can either demonstrate all of the criteria that constitute that outcome, or you can't . . . *yet*. And if you can't yet, well OK, there's more learning to do until you finally can. No grading on a curve in ink, lemon Lexuses, or Cs in algebra!

Yes, we know, the Grading/Marking B⌐X is profoundly entrenched in the mind-set of Western civilization, but that doesn't make it valid. It makes it a misguided habit! There's no such thing as a C+ merit badge in the Scouts, or a B– black belt in karate, or a D in commercial pilot licensing . . . or in any other kind of demonstration of learning that's criterion-defined. (If pilots went to educentric schools, they could fail the unit on "Landing" and still pass the course called "Piloting"!) So none of these familiar examples, and countless others like them, operates within the educentric paradigm. They're all examples of real-life performance abilities. And they're much more concrete, much easier to explain, and much easier to justify than letter grades.

Hence, MCL promotes and documents actual demonstrations of each learner's work in the form of electronic portfolio "exhibits." In some cases, this may be as simple as identifying the learning outcome/objective and showing the written documentation of the learner demonstrating his or her mastery of it. In other cases, it may be as complex as a learner using multimedia to demonstrate the outcome "persuasion through logic and rationale" in advocating the adoption of a future-focused curriculum before his local board of education. (This is an actual learner experience that, according to news reports, won the debate but not the vote of the board majority.)

Given the capacity of today's hard drives and the ingenuity of today's learners, there's no end to what can be placed in an electronic portfolio. But portfolios must be organized and targeted to be influential. Just forwarding megabytes of stuff to someone is probably not going to impress. But once well-defined data have been entered and "tagged," they can be retrieved in a number of formats and used in a number of ways. (Here we strongly recommend that you read *Everything Is Miscellaneous* by David Weinberger.) The very same "tagged" data, with the push of a button, can reorganize an electronic portfolio and make it available

- In chronological order of accomplishment

- Organized by life-performance learner outcomes

- Organized by sphere of living outcomes

- By the format in which it's stored . . . Word, PowerPoint, Excel, audio, video, et cetera

- According to traditional subject areas . . . English, math, social studies, et cetera

- In college application format

- In job application format, and/or

- Any other organizer you might choose

If you thought you could impress your neighbor over the back fence with your kid's GPA, well, just wait till she whips out her 2012 iPhone and lays her kid's electronic portfolio demo at Carnegie Hall on you—video and ear buds included!

Electronic Portfolios Extended

And yes, for those who are into comparison and ranking, electronic portfolios could also provide up-to-date data regarding a learner's

- Ranking for his or her age group

- Achievement expectation considering IQ

- Ranking as to workweek hours

- Achievement compared with specific college admissions standards

- Achievement ranking when compared to other athletes/band members/students, and/or

- Any other criterion they might create

We're not suggesting that this be done out of fear that these rankings might simply take the place of GPA rankings. We're only alerting you to the potential that lies within today's technologies. Whether to go this far down the "comparison path" is a decision your ELC will have to make, but the social/cultural inertia around ranking may be difficult to resist.

A Learner's MCL Experience

With almost everything we've described in this book so far taken into account, here's how it all translates in terms of a learner's experience. This example relates to a high school situation, since it's most in need of

MCL-type change. Our hypothetical student is Lori, and she's creating her learning schedule for a two-month period.

- Lori is fourteen years old, a "good kid," is into music and sports, and has three or four close girlfriends that she hangs out with.

- Lori is a rather responsible, self-directed learner . . . but a teenager!

- Lori has a learning coach whom she helped to select.

- Lori has access to a computer and the Internet in her home.

- Lori's ELC has created the expectation that parents will be involved in the creation and monitoring of their child's learning schedule.

Lori's learning coach must approve Lori's learning schedule, and at least one of her parents is required to be involved in her scheduling conference. However, Lori, not her learning coach, is responsible for leading this three-way conference—a huge step out of the Role/Control B☐X! Her learning profile, her demonstrated responsibility, and her ELC's mission of "creating self-directed, lifelong learners," makes this a prudent, constructive decision. In fact, it might not even be necessary for her learning coach to be there because she'll get an e-mail detailing Lori's proposed schedule, and she could be involved later if she thinks modifications are in order.

But what if Lori were not a responsible learner? Who would be leading the conference then? Probably her learning coach. But the ELC's goal for each learner is for them to become self-directed learners, and both the staff and parents should be intentional about making that happen.

For this process to work, Lori's ELC must have selected and installed scheduling technology consistent with our sixth critical "ready for rollout" component noted earlier. It would allow for two key things: (1) learners creating their individual schedules based on a master schedule of predetermined learning opportunities and activities, and (2) individual learner decisions being communicated in real time to everyone with "a need to know." (Microsoft's Exchange ActiveSync, for example, has electronic calendars that now do this for individuals, teams, and organizations.)

Scheduling Priorities

As Lori thinks of all of the things she wants to do and accomplish in the next two months, she realizes that some activities are set in time and can't be adjusted, while others are flexible and can. Gymnastics practice, for example, is on a set schedule for all varsity gymnasts, but working through math outcomes online can be scheduled at her discretion. So Lori first places gymnastics, her most inflexible activity, on her schedule each day from 3:30 p.m. to 5:30 p.m. This happens in a matter of seconds.

The next least flexible thing on Lori's list of learning activities is the "interactive seminars" she wants to attend, and so she schedules them next. Depending on the outcomes she wants to address and strengthen over the next two months, she'll probably select and apply for five or six of them. Since Lori wants to attend the interpersonal communications seminar, she locates it online on the ELC's listing of seminar offerings and finds that it's a thirty-hour, highly interactive experience that is scheduled for three hours each morning, Monday through Friday for two weeks, from 8:30 to 11:30 a.m. She finds the two-week timeframe that seems to best fit her needs and places it on her schedule.

If there's an opening in that seminar, she'll automatically be registered. But if it's full, she'll be alerted to the interpersonal communications seminars that do have openings. (Typical of fourteen-year-old girls, Lori will probably have talked all of this over with her friends in advance, and they'll do their best to work/manipulate the system to get into the same section.) She'll then schedule the rest of her seminars in a like manner, and will probably have to rearrange some previous decisions to make everything work for her.

The MCL Scheduling Sequence
(from the least to the most flexible)

1. Team sports/music (e.g., gymnastics, band)
2. Interactive seminars (e.g., Interpersonal Communications)
3. Co-op learning online (e.g., math online, learning with three friends)
4. Personal learning interests/projects (e.g., economics of the music world)
5. Personal online learning objectives/outcomes (e.g., math, U.S. history)

After she completes her entire two-month schedule and hits "Send," Lori's gymnastics coach, her learning coach, her seminar facilitators, her parents, and her ELC's head are all officially informed of Lori's intentions/schedule. In response, her seminar facilitators will send her an invitation to each seminar along with a listing of things she is to read/study prior to starting.

Additional Learning Alternatives

Because Lori is well aware of her ELC's life performance outcomes and the enabling outcomes and curriculum objectives that underlie them, she has the flexibility of addressing specific outcomes in a variety of ways. Therefore, she may negotiate with her learning coach to do a personal project instead of attending an interactive seminar or addressing that outcome online.

For example, if there were an outcome that required Lori to be able to create and defend a complex business plan, and if she had a strong interest in the economics of the music industry, she would be free to pursue that line of interest. One alternative she could consider is to shadow/be mentored by the manager of a retail music store, and/or by the agent of a well-known performer in the community. If that seemed feasible to her learning coach, she would have the responsibility of working it out. In the end, it's the demonstration of learning that counts, and the intrinsic motivation is there when the learner also has an interest in the content.

The remainder of Lori's learning schedule, although concerning very important learner outcomes, can also be filled at her discretion. She has a great deal of flexibility regarding when she will learn the over 50 percent of the curriculum that can best be learned online—and online here is truly 24/7/365. That gets filled in last in her schedule, and she can pursue these outcomes/objectives at home, on her own during the day, or collaboratively with her friends. All of them will be assessed individually, of course, but they're free to help each other's learning progress. When her schedule is fully completed, she can again hit "Send," and all the relevant parties will be further informed about her learning endeavors for the next two months.

ELCs are free to set controls when and where they need to for learners who've proven themselves to be not as responsible as Lori. Less responsible learners might be required to do their online work in a supervised computer lab, for example, and have a meeting with their learning coach prior to leaving each day until they can clearly demonstrate greater personal responsibility for their learning.

Letting the Fast Runners Run

The two most memorable and most costly federal initiatives of our time were the ESEA Act of 1965 and the No Child Left Behind legislation of today. Both of these initiatives had, and continue to have, a significant impact on local decision making. Each of these federal programs targeted the real needs of learners who were not achieving, and we are certainly not here to argue against that focus on underachievers. But in the process, we have not served the "fast runners" well. Be clear: Our position is not an either/or position; it is a both/and position.

There was/is a little money for the gifted and talented in the ESEA Act of 1965, but that allocation usually financed only small "pullout" programs, often based purely on standard measures of IQ. This made it clear to informed educators that there was no research-based definition of "gifted and talented." The truth is that we really can't identify gifted and talented children at an early age, even though parents and grandparents seem to be able to: They all have them! And, in fact, if we were to ask the question right, "*How* is little Julie talented?" based on what we described in chapter 3, they all are talented.

So even if we can't identify or agree on who's gifted, we can identify the fast runners. They make up about 25 percent of our learners, and they're the ones getting As, taking AP courses, and asking for extra credit work. Our industrial age instructional delivery system limits their potential with a glass (or maybe steel) ceiling. If your high schools offer one high-level math class per year, your best learners could leave with only four math credits. MCL, however, would make calculus and beyond a strong possibility for mathematically adept fast runners.

MCL encourages "continuous progress," allowing the highly motivated, hard-working, high achievers the opportunity to move at their own rate—and with little or no additional cost to the system. Imagine what would happen to those comparative international achievement test results if we'd let our fast runners run. Our bet is that our higher level achievement test scores would "smoke" those of South Korea and Singapore (who just happen to be better at the industrial age than we are—or if we stated it a little more sarcastically, "better at being obsolete than we are").

Assessing Your ELC's Readiness for MCL

Here's Your MCL Readiness Test:

Can you describe MCL in a way that convinces secondary school principals that they can fully implement MCL and still remain "in control" of their school?

When working with leadership teams and having six to ten hours to present, discuss, and clarify MCL's ten weight-bearing walls, we get real about the above test. Although MCL should be applied at all levels of the system, it seems to fit secondary schools the best, and it's where we think it's most needed. Secondary principals must be able to "control" their schools. Control certainly isn't a negative word in this regard. Show us a secondary principal who can't control his or her school, and we'll show you an ex–secondary principal.

So, should we feel confident when, after explaining MCL to secondary principals and asking them if MCL is doable, they'll respond with a yes? Well, we always do—and it's usually an enthusiastic one. And why shouldn't we get a yes? MCL is logical and rational, it meets the needs of students much better than what we are doing now, it allows for the consistent application of our best research regarding motivation and learning, and all the transformational technology necessary to roll it out is available and tested. It's a wonderful example of cross-industry learning, and it opens the door to genuine and deep restructuring.

So please consider that any "restructuring" that retains the educentric assembly line and most of the fifteen boxes isn't real restructuring. We're fooling ourselves if we think so . . . and maybe others, too. The future of education is far too important to not rid ourselves of a structure designed for a world that is over a hundred years gone. The assembly line doesn't fit our world nor does it fit the learning needs of our children. Were children politically powerful adults, they wouldn't put up with it.

We've learned over the decades that the only way we can stop the assembly line is to stop the assembly line. We can't rename it, dance around it, ask teachers to do the impossible in classrooms with thirty-plus diverse learners while administrators hide behind the administrative convenience of an outdated bureaucracy. Transformation requires deep change, deep change requires risk, and risk requires courage ("cojones," if you wish). MCL provides the best opportunity for structural transformation, with the backing and use of some of the best technologies around. Its face will no doubt change as educators drop the assembly line and continuously improve on and refine its implementation. But it's the *place* to start, and *now*'s the time!

BUILDING AN ALIGNED SUPPORT STRUCTURE

The main thing is to *keep* the main thing the main thing!

How badly do you want it?

The highlighted components of figures 7.1 and 7.2 on the next page contain the word "support." Your organizational vision is inspirational, its direction is clear, the empowered self-directed lifelong learners you want to send out the door to meet the challenges and opportunities of Empowermentland have been defined and described, and you're planning to restructure your learning system around mass customized learning. You've got a beautiful picture of an ELC here. So how badly do you want it?

Alignment: Prerequisite to Effectiveness

Structural alignment. Intentionally creating organizational structures, functions, processes, and practices to accomplish the organization's purpose and vision.

People alignment. Focusing the attitudes, energy, expertise, and efforts of all staff members on the organization's purpose and vision.

If you want it with all your heart and soul, you'll begin aligning your ELC's support structure with every other component we've described so far . . . actually before the ink is dry on your transformational philosophy and learner outcomes documents. And you'll never let up. That's what

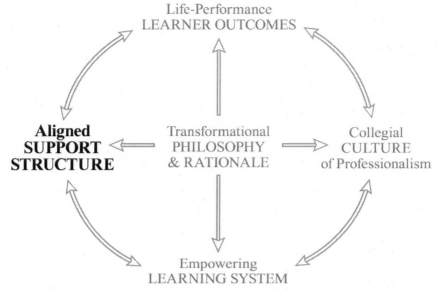

Life-Performance
LEARNER OUTCOMES

**Aligned
SUPPORT
STRUCTURE**

Transformational
PHILOSOPHY
& RATIONALE

Collegial
CULTURE
of Professionalism

Empowering
LEARNING SYSTEM

Figure 7.1.   Focusing on an ELC's support structure.

VISIONARY
Creative & Cutting Edge
Vision

SERVICE
Compassionate
& Dedicated
Support

AUTHENTIC
Conscious
& Ethical
Purpose

RELATIONAL
Collaborative
& Collegial
Ownership

QUALITY
Competent & Expert
Capacity

Figure 7.2.   The parallel emphasis of Total Leadership 2.0.

successful implementation takes—and explicit, direct, and total alignment is the only way to make it happen. This means that every person, every resource, every technology, every process, every procedure, and every policy must be aligned and harmonious with each other. Anything not aligned with this overall vision must be redirected, and anyone not enthusiastically supporting the vision must be confronted.

If this sounds tough, it is, because we've really reached the "heavy-lifting" aspect of leadership and change. You could argue that up to this point we've been describing highly inspiring and empowering things you "should" do if you really want to create/implement/lead a genuine ELC. Well, here we are at "crunch" time. Do you really want to create and lead the ELC vision described so far? It's action time, and the Service Leader 2.0 really must be "in service" to the vision you've established in doing the work described in chapters 2 through 5 and the major restructuring spelled out in chapter 6. If you haven't taken these steps, or are concerned about doing so, then this chapter may only hold "informational"—rather than "directional"—value for you.

So please stop, consider the significance of what you are about to undertake, reflect deeply on your professional and personal life purposes, and answer the question:

Am I willing to do the hard work, take the risks, spend my chits, and risk failure to make this vision of an ELC happen?

If your answer is a sincere and enthusiastic yes, this chapter will offer lots of practical advice. But, as you've no doubt surmised, creating change of this depth and magnitude won't be a cakewalk.

Really Shifting the Paradigm!

Yes, we're back to the subject of paradigms again, not because we have little else to say, but precisely because we have even more to say. And it needs to heard, viewed, and acted upon like a Total Leader 2.0 would:

- As a future-focused professional, not an educentric bureaucrat

- As a service-oriented leader, not a convenience-oriented administrator

- As a learner-centered educator, not a convention-driven manager

- As an empowering human being, not a controlling one

We've discussed these profound differences numerous times throughout the book, and now it's time to turn them into action—the "doing" side of the paradigm, not just its "viewing" side. As we argued extensively in chapter 2, both the viewing and the doing in education are severely constrained by its century of bureaucratic inertia—inertia that's been present and perpetuated since any of us first hit school at age five. In bureaucracies, the three Rs prevail: regulations, routines, and rituals. Human beings, whether called customers, clients, students, learners, or staff are compelled to give way to these organizational "imperatives."

Whether you call them the fifteen boxes or the three Rs, these alleged imperatives create what we all know as "comfort zones"—psychological and operational places where we can count on things happening a given way because they always have and, presumably, always will. So when you just said yes to really wanting to create the kind of ELC we've been describing, you're choosing to directly confront the bureaucratic comfort-zone essence of education. Why? Because it's held in place by an aligned support structure too, made up of boxes, Rs, and the acquiescence of the organization's participants.

So the essence of this chapter is a request from us to you: Completely redefine the support structure on which your ELC's learning system depends! Right now the decisions, actions, infrastructure, resources, recognition, and rewards being provided to education continue to support and reinforce the bureaucracy. We're asking that that powerful configuration of factors be redefined and redirected to support and reinforce learner empowerment instead. Anything less will be swept away on the next high tide of institutional/bureaucratic inertia.

Transformational Technologies as Support Resources

Chapter 6 provided a great example of support structure power. You saw that learner-centered instruction that is powerful, empowering, and just plain smart is inseparable from the adept use of today's transformational technologies. Those technologies are part of your support structure, and they give you the capacity to transform your ELC's learning system. Without them, mass customized learning (or any other comprehensive model of personalized learning) just couldn't operate. But unless you train your ELC's staff to use them effectively, the technologies are no more than a silver lever that can't be pulled.

So investing in both the technologies and the training to use them is something that ELCs must do if they hope to break the assembly-line mold and truly become learner-centered. And Service Leaders 2.0 are the first to see that is has to be done, then decide that it is going to be done, and then work with their people so that it gets done . . . and done well. In the case of MCL, this means replacing ten entrenched educentric weight-bearing walls with learner-centered empowering ones. It sounds daunting, but if you plan for it, prepare your people for it, allocate time and resources to introducing and developing it, and engage your people in implementing it, it can and will happen. That's what we mean by aligning your support structure with your new vision!

Typical Processes and Functions Requiring Alignment

All organizations are unique to some degree, but from our experience in facilitating change efforts, the following list provides a good start in identifying those important processes and functions in educational entities that typically will need realignment:

1. Curriculum development

2. The instructional delivery system

3. Student assessment and placement

4. Staff selection and assignment

5. Staff development

6. Organizational culture

7. Instructional technology

8. Information technology

9. The budget process

10. Labor relations

11. The transportation operation

12. The maintenance department

13. The food service operation

14. School board support

15. Community involvement and support

All organizations are managed and controlled by a number of processes, functions, procedures, and practices like these, and someone in the organization is charged with the leadership and operation of each of them. Each of these leaders/managers must be clear about your ELC's new learner-centered vision and aware of what he or she must do to align his or her function to support it. This requires the orientations and skills of the Service Leader 2.0—someone who helps everyone in the organization know the importance of alignment and support; who monitors its systems and functions to ensure that the support is forthcoming; and who empowers, coaches, and rewards supportive contributions to the organization's vision.

To comprehensively and systematically align your support structure with the new vision, you should take great care to identify and align the particularly influential processes and functions that would probably go unnoticed by those not directly involved in instruction. Below are three examples from these fifteen that highlight this important point and illustrate the kind of alignment/support that's going to be required.

First, here's how an aligned budget process might unfold:

1. Those responsible for developing the ELC's budget can enthusiastically articulate, and are openly committed to, the ELC's learner-centered vision.

2. The business office systematically uses the vision as a decision screen as they create the budget, and again when they authorize expenditures.

3. The budget effectively communicates the ELC's purpose, priorities, and vision to the staff and other stakeholders. Its

structure and line item amounts directly reflect the ELC's mission, values, and vision.

4. The budget-planning process encourages and includes input from, and interaction with, all learning facilitators and other stakeholders.

5. The resulting budget provides sufficient resources for the effective and efficient implementation of its vision.

Second, you've probably come across a transportation director or two who operated as though schools exist to serve the bus schedule. Well, those people are going to have to both expand and transform their department's mission—from "operating busses that pick up and deliver students safely to their school and back on a set schedule" to "transporting learners to and from learning sites safely and 'ready to learn' throughout the day as their needs require." In other words, they'll have to think and act like managers of city transportation systems who help people come and go at all hours—not as schedule-driven bureaucrats.

Third, all organizations have a process for recruiting and selecting staff members, and, in the case of teachers, this is tantamount to making a twenty-five-year decision! Therefore, if the personnel department is not aligned with the vision, they could easily continue to hire teachers who are deeply in love with their area of expertise but who generally view students as chair fillers—human containers to be filled with their favorite knowledge and wisdom. By contrast, being learner-centered requires instructional facilitators who recognize and honor the uniqueness of each learner and, in fact, who explore learners' areas of interest with them. This is the difference between "the sage on the stage" and "the guide on the side." ELCs need way more guides than sages.

You, Modeling the New Paradigm and Vision

Imagine the power of having all fifteen functions and processes listed above aligned with your inspirational, future-focused, learner-centered vision. The morning after the board approves the life performance learner outcomes (chapter 4) and the empowered learning system vision (chapters 5 and 6), expect to be facilitating a meeting that includes all staff members responsible for curriculum, instruction, learner assessment, instructional technology, and information technology. If you modeled your meeting agenda after a TL2.0's, it would probably read like this:

1. My total commitment to our vision—it's OK to test me on this.

2. My ninety-second "elevator speech" describing the vision—please work on yours.

3. Support of our vision requires a team approach. You are the varsity—the players that most influence the learner experience.

4. Total commitment is required and expected. I want you here, but if you can't buy in, we need to talk.

5. Your role: Do you know it? We will clarify as we go.

6. Let's begin with your vision for your function: Can we expect a draft for our Monday meeting? Your vision should clearly show how your function will support/be aligned with our vision. I have some ideas if you want them.

7. Technology whiz: Can you bring a plan for how our team can operate and communicate with each other and with our stakeholders as we work together on our vision?

8. I will be accessible. Our new vision is my/our "priority one."

Now here's a leadership meeting we'd love to attend, because it emphasizes the overwhelming importance of building key staff support for your new vision and for giving it immediate and direct legitimacy!

Getting Everyone on the "Systematic Alignment" Bus

In his highly acclaimed book *Good to Great*, Jim Collins offers very sound advice when he states that "Level 5" leaders "get the right people on the bus, the wrong people off the bus, and the right people in the right seats."

In a nutshell, that's a key purpose of the service leader and also the mission of your ELC's personnel department.

To reinforce Collins's point, please note that we work with business and industry as well as education entities, and we experience their follow-through on strategic designs and/or new visions to be quite different. Business is much more likely to quickly implement a new strategic direction and vision than is education. Business employees know their supervisors will have expectations of them, and so they get informed and they readily get involved in making the expected changes. Their participation doesn't always reflect strong commitment—there are the occasional sarcastic remarks regarding leadership—but real follow-through on a plan is the norm.

But school systems don't work that way. While business employees are apt to look at a new vision and say, "What does this mean for me?" educators frequently look at a new vision and say, "Some good ideas here . . . but they're optional." In the case of your ELC's collectively created strategic direction and vision for its learners, however, there's nothing about it that's optional. Meaningful change is hard enough when everyone is committed, but it's nearly impossible when a significant part of the staff resists getting on the bus and is allowed to stay off.

Our "Supervision for Alignment" Process

Our experience strongly indicates that if educational leaders don't openly, systematically, and forcefully create a system to ensure that everyone—yes, everyone—gets on the vision bus, it won't become a reality. There will be too many boxes to cling to, too many comfort zones to hide in, and too much inertia to drag along. Realizing that this was true, we created a process called "Supervision for Alignment" that ensures that everyone gets on the bus and takes a seat. We've implemented it in a number of school systems, and it's had a very positive impact on the likelihood of organizational follow-through—follow-through that makes the work of "deriving life performance learner outcomes" and "implementing an empowering learning system" well worth the effort. (Note: We're not trying to "sell" you our Supervision for Alignment workshop. We're using it here as an example of what service leaders must do to ensure everyone's active participation.)

You're certainly free to create or use your own process—but know that if you don't have a process that gets systematically implemented, many will see the new vision as an option, and things will stall.

Briefly, Supervision for Alignment (S4A) is a process for leaders at all levels of an organization that we present in a workshop format. The process equips them with a method for ensuring that there is close alignment between

- The values, motivations, and activities of those they supervise, and

- The values, mission, and vision of the organization

S4A is totally transparent. Everyone in the organization is given the twelve "dialogue starters" that leaders learn to work with in the workshop. And they're also given the response that the supervisor will be listening for. Since this is neither a "gotcha" exercise nor an evaluation, the dialogue is intended to be as stress free as possible. The dialogue *is* designed, however, to help everyone know their role in actualizing the organization's empowering vision, and it works when every supervisor systematically conducts this dialogue with all of their reports.

Nearly every leader in an organization is a linking pin—that is, they're a member of one group and a leader of another. If any one leader does not follow through with the S4A process, they are allowing anyone below them on their "supervision chart" to take a pass. Hence, in the typical school district we suggest that a committee of the board conduct the dialogue with the superintendent, that the superintendent conduct the dialogue with each of his or her reports, and so on throughout the entire system.

The Dialogue Starters

The first dialogue starter is the most critical. We suggest that the S4A process be done with each person at least twice each year, and this first question will always be the kickoff of the process. Everyone will soon learn that this first question is going to be asked, and many may begin answering it before the supervisor even asks it. All dialogue starters follow this format:

Question 1 is about alignment—

How does your work relate to achieving the core values, the mission, and the vision of our organization?

Its Rationale. This question (1) focuses the supervision process on the implementation of the organization's strategic direction, (2) helps align the achievements and growth opportunities of individuals with the focus of the system, and (3) clearly signals everyone that they are responsible for implementing the organization's core values, mission, and vision.

The Desired Response. Respondents are able to describe how significant aspects of their work align with and support the values, mission, and vision.

The Supervisor's Prompt. "Let's look at some of your significant work and compare it with our values, mission, and vision."

The Supervisor's Teaching Opportunity. "Let's take some time to talk about our core values, mission, and vision and see how they can be used as a decision screen for what happens."

Note that all the dialogue starters begin with a question. That question does not have to be stated verbatim and can be paraphrased in a vocabulary common to the relationship, but the substance and intent of the question must be retained. Each dialogue starter also provides a rationale for the question, the generally desired response, a prompt should the person need help, and a teaching opportunity if the supervisee doesn't understand the concept in question—all very transparent. Typically, the process seems a bit clumsy the first time through the dialogues. But after eighteen months and three S4A sessions, understanding, ease, and momentum increase to the point that the first dialogue starter may well be answered:

> **"Our vision has become my job description.**
> **It's the focus of nearly everything I do."**

The S4S process continues with:

- Three questions about *success*—questions that allow the person to share their successes, identify the talents that created the successes, and possibilities for transferring these talents to other job challenges or opportunities.

- Three questions about *quality*—questions that help supervisees identify their quality standards, identify their feedback loops, and allow them to tell the supervisor what he or she can do to make them even more successful in ensuring quality.

- Three questions about *vision*—questions that allow supervisees to share their expectations of future conditions, share their vision for his area of responsibility, and allow them to tell the supervisor what he or she can do to help them achieve their vision.

- A question about *personal values*—and whether they are aligned with those of the organization and whether discrepancies might exist.

- A question about the *S4A process*—how it is working for the person, and what the organization can do to improve it for them.

This process may seem time consuming given all of the other things that leaders have to do, but a TL2.0 would disagree. For the TL2.0, S4A is not "something else I have to do. It's the essence of my job!" Truly, both quality leadership and service leadership as we define them in *TL2.0* require a supervision process that empowers everyone to do their part in making the organization's vision come to life.

The Service Leader as Talent Scout, and More

Education is a people business. So attracting, selecting, contracting, orienting, developing, empowering, rewarding, retaining, advancing, and sometimes out-counseling people is a leader's Job One. You may wish to read this last sentence again slowly, as it sequentially lists ten things that the gurus of the leadership literature consistently identify as an organization's critical personnel processes. Executing them intelligently and thoroughly is fundamental to building and implementing an aligned support structure. Some of these ten processes have been with us for a long time, but others on the list have arrived with the age of empowerment.

Personnel Recruitment: "Threes Are Us!"

Recruitment used to be initiated by announcing an opening in a state-sponsored job placement service. Not so today. Smart service leaders realize that successful recruitment starts with their ELC's image/reputation/"brand." So, what's your ELC's brand? Are you the Pittsburgh Steelers of ELCs, the Dallas Cowboys, or the Oakland Raiders? Each brand attracts a different type of person. Do you want to play for a winner or do you want to make a loser a winner?

High-reputation ELCs attract people who are learner-centered, future-focused, lifelong learning professionals. To be specific, they—and you—should be speaking the language and sending out "signals" that resonate strongly with the people Renate and Geoffrey Caine (see chapter 5) call Perceptual Orientation Threes, the masters of learner-centered instruction. They're big-picture thinkers with an empowering approach to life and their work. And, as we noted there, they exhibit higher levels of our five wellsprings (consciousness, creativity, collaboration, competence, and compassion) than do Ones (the masters of direct instruction) and Twos (strong content specialists), and they thrive on big-picture discourse.

On the other hand, Plain Jane school systems project themselves in standard educentric/bureaucratic ways and tend to attract people who are looking for a job. Sometimes this attracts Twos and some Threes, but mostly it doesn't. So they end up with lots of in-the-box Ones. Service Leaders 2.0 don't leave such a critical matter to chance. They know their brand and proudly promote it. You might say their motto is "Threes Are Us!"

Non-Educentric Personnel Selection

The selection process in ELCs has also changed significantly, and along these very same lines. Real ELCs no longer simply look for people with the legal qualifications, high college GPAs, and "good papers"—what education generally regards as "solid"/able people. They now seek applicants who have talents, attitudes, beliefs, and values that match their transformational vision and their empowerment mission—professionals who believe that education is the world's most important profession and every learner counts.

They want competence and skills too, of course, but the guideline for the day is to hire for qualities and attitude, teach for skills. Good professional development programs can teach competencies, but they can't teach qualities, attitude, and talent. Translate that into what we just said about Perceptual Orientation Threes, the five wellsprings, and the empowering qualities ELCs are seeking to promote in their learners: self-directed, self-assessing, self-governing, and self-renewing contributors. In short, they're looking for good people who embody and project their vision in who they are, and how they function. In that light, GPAs pale by comparison.

Paradigm-Shifting Personnel Development

An ELC's approach to what is traditionally called "staff development" needs to embody and model its vision for learners. To us this means that staff members need to see themselves as empowered role performers in the same way that the ELC's life-performance outcomes define their vision for learners: As, for example,

Empowered, ethical HUMANS

Eclectic, visionary THINKERS and INNOVATORS

Respectful, responsible COMMUNICATORS and
TEAM MEMBERS

Resourceful, responsible IMPLEMENTERS and PERFORMERS

Discerning, supportive ADVOCATES and CONTRIBUTORS

. . . a framework we've borrowed from chapter 4. This approach encourages staff to self-assess where they're operating at the One, Two, or Three level (for example), identify where they can target areas of personal and professional growth, and translate these insights into a learning/development plan that can be guided and monitored by an "implementation coach" whom they can select from a common pool of experienced facilitators.

This personalized/customized approach needs to have as its grounding the major paradigm shift elements we highlighted in chapters 1 and 5. If you need a refresher on this critical framework, you'll find it in the latter part of chapter 1 and near the beginning of chapter 5. Its elements need to be part of both your new non-educentric professional development focus, and its regular mode of discourse.

And while the entire thrust of this book is about awakening and honoring the inherent internal motivation of human beings, we also believe in this case that your ELC would be wise to establish some kind of incentive system for staff who involve themselves in continuous growth and development activities of this kind. And here we want to reinforce the word "continuous." In an ELC, no one is ever "done" learning, growing, and expanding who they are and what they can contribute to others' learning, growth, and expansion.

Proactive Personnel Empowerment

Empowerment was once regarded as the latest buzzword, but as we pointed out many times in *TL2.0*, it's proven itself to be the critical factor in maximizing both individual and team performance. TL2.0s know that "empowered people produce." Business leaders know it from watching the bottom line, and education leaders know it by watching for creativity, innovation, hard work, and highly motivated people.

TL2.0s don't wait for people to ask for empowerment; they recruit for it, select for it, model it, develop for it, supervise for it, and expect it of everyone. Again, let's reinforce this point with the words we used above: their constant focus is on, self-directed, self-assessing, self-governing, and self-renewing contributors.

Active Personnel Retention

In today's age of empowerment, retaining good people isn't what it used to be. As we pointed out several times in *TL2.0*, creative and talented employees have many options, and they're not afraid to exercise them. Salary is a major factor in business, but it is only a key attractor that initially gets good people in the door. What keeps talented people there is if they're given meaningful work, empowered to do things the way they think is best, are members of a talented congenial team, are recognized for their contributions, are encouraged to continue to learn and grow, and are given special perks that make their life easier and more exciting. (Google even allows its people to bring their pets to work!)

Since salaries in education are severely constrained and limited through standardized contractual arrangements, leaders typically can do little to provide direct financial enhancements to their strongest contributors. However, there's a powerful lesson for them here in how to create positive and compelling non-financial inducements for their Threes. Threes are looking for a great place to work and to be recognized for what they contribute. Please respond accordingly!

Enlightened Out-Counseling

**In his best-seller *Good to Great*,
Jim Collins says this about "Level 5" leaders:**

They "get the right people on the bus, the wrong people off the bus, and the right people in the right seats."

Yes, getting the wrong people off of the bus is the unpleasant part of Jim Collins's three-part statement, and educators do it poorly and rarely. Our systems hurt because of this, our learners hurt because of this, our profession hurts because of this, and ELCs can't really function properly because of this.

Since they tend to be caring, supportive, and positive people, it's very difficult for educational policy makers and leaders to remove non-aligned and marginally performing colleagues (be they superintendents, specialists, principals, or teachers). In fact, many leaders were hired specifically because they had those qualities. But we're not letting them off scot-free here; there are ways of out-counseling marginal employees and doing it while keeping their dignity intact. The process requires both skill and will—and will seems to be the hardest to come by.

No, "out-counseling" isn't the same as "doing a Donald Trump" with an assertive statement: "You're fired!" Yet the out-counseling leader must be clear that non-aligned, underperforming people cannot remain in their positions. They are undermining the efforts of everyone else in what must be a cohesive, empowering organizational culture. Fair and caring leaders will sincerely work with them to help them find a position in or outside of education more suited to their particular attitudes, skills, and work ethic, and that's a critical element in what we mean by "enlightened" out-counseling.

Happily, we've developed a hands-on workshop of processes and skills that make out-counseling the marginal employee less painful for both the supervisor and supervisee. The process requires good interpersonal skills, writing/documentation skills, knowledge of personnel laws and regulations and your organization's policies, and the advice of an attorney with experience in personnel and due process law. If the candor, potential confrontations, and emotions inherent in out-counseling appear to be difficult for you, you may wish to learn about it from someone who has been in that situation a few times and can share some do's and don'ts with you.

When Tenure Doesn't Support Professionalism

We can't go into detail regarding tenure and due process laws here, but teacher employment contracts have come to be abused, and they're the curse of educational change. Why? Because they're grounded in the industrial age, written in industrial age language, and foster and reinforce industrial age assembly-line thinking and practices. And please understand, this candid observation does not make us anti-teacher; it makes us pro-empowerment and pro-professional. We're about honoring and empowering those teachers who strive to be more than their employment contract demands—in fact, who break the contractual mold to truly serve their learners.

We know that this analogy has its limits, but there is a remarkable parallel between what's happening in education and what's happened to General Motors. Both suffer(ed) under four similar burdens: (1) a lack of decisive visionary leadership, (2) oppressive union contracts, (3) a continuing loss of market share, and (4) a closed-system culture of "we've always done it this way before, and the country can't get along without us." Yes, GM had to be closed down and reconstituted in 2009 because the convergence of these four factors made it difficult to be creative, to change, to be competitive, and to meet customer needs.

But way before then, GM (like public education) didn't have to be competitive; Chrysler and Ford had the same unions so the playing field was level. But that was decades ago, before real competition, globalization, the quality paradigm, and high gas prices hit.

Decisively Managing Your ELC's Many Resources

Our definition of organizational "resources" is much broader than that of the traditional manager. Dollars and technologies may be the most tangible of resources, but there are other leader-controlled resources that can be even more impactful. We're encouraging you to add the following to your roster of resources that can be appropriately aligned and allocated to support your ELC's empowering learning system:

- **Time**. There is just so much of it on your calendar, and we're urging you to use it to enhance the accomplishment of your ELC's vision as priority one. Service Leaders monitor their agenda and calendar to ensure that they're devoting time to what truly supports their learning system's effectiveness and success. If that means choosing between coaching a teacher about how to better use the ELC's transformational technologies or having coffee with a board member, she'll do the coaching. For perspectives on managing the ELC's time and talent, we urge you to revisit chapter 6.

- **Focus**. Yes, focused attention is a resource. You may be good at multitasking, but there can only be one focus, only one decision screen running in your mind at a time. Service leaders are not "generalists"; they are specialists at consistently focusing everyone's attention, priorities, and decision making on the organization's vision . . . including their own. As one of Bill's favorite slides says: "If Everything is your priority, then Nothing is your priority!"

- **Learning**. Self-directed, lifelong learners enjoy learning things as and when the spirit moves them. But when they have their Service Leader 2.0 hat on and are responsible for creating the changes required in their ELC's new vision, their learning becomes focused on what it takes to make the vision happen. For example, there is probably more to learn about customizing learning by analyzing how iTunes customizes music delivery than there is by reading a variety of articles in *The School Administrator* or *Educational Leadership*. And the same holds for organizational learning. Staff reading and discussions should be equally well focused on what it truly means to be a "learning organization."

- **Rewards**. Bonuses, common in business, are not part of the culture of school systems, where egalitarianism trumps meritocracy. But service leaders have a host of intangible rewards to distribute, including: meaningful work, recognition for contributions made, being part of a highly effective team, being challenged while being empowered, expanded opportunities for professional participation and growth, and so on. And they come without political cost to the committed Service Leader 2.0.

- **The Community**. The people, service organizations, and businesses in a community can be viewed as a public relations chore or as a valuable element in an aligned support system. From the earliest stages of planning for strategic design to the implementation of the vision, smart TL2.0s engage everyone with an interest and stake in their ELC's success in participating—both to shape its vision and to actively support it on the ground. In so doing, they make community members advocates for the vision and, when appropriate, hosts and learning facilitators for community-based learning projects. This way "Our community is a world of learning opportunities" becomes more than a slogan on a banner in their ELC's entranceways.

The Issue of Resource Equity

Typically, managers are careful to distribute resources, be it money or time, "fairly." If they have a $2000 travel budget for the four English teachers in their school, then "fairly" sounds like each teacher should receive $500 of that budget. Or if they dropped an "attaboy" note into one teacher's mailbox, they'd sure better send notes to the others lest they be seen as playing favorites. The paradox here is that service leaders, being firm that they're in service to the organization's vision, don't think or operate this way.

Yes, we used the term "heavy lifting" at the beginning of the chapter, noting the "hard" work service leaders have to do to really "make change happen." And this applies more than anything to how they will allocate the resources at their disposal. Their priority one: Making the vision happen. This means that travel requests that have to do with learning how technology can be used to customize learning opportunities will be approved, but requests to attend the state English teachers' conference may not be. In their sometimes "lonely" world of aligned decision making that sometimes turns comfort zones upside down, both tangible and intangible rewards go to those committed to and focused on the ELC's empowering values, mission, and vision.

Your Impact and Legacy

In short, chapters 4, 5, and 6 represent bold visions regarding the purpose and the structure of ELCs. If you believe in, and are passionate about, this vision and what it will do for your learners, if you have the will and courage to take the risk and to "go for it," and if you follow the experientially gained advice that we've offered throughout this book, we're confident that you, a newly emerging TL2.0, will make a contribution to shaping the future of education that has been sorely needed for many decades. Your steadfastness in breaking out of the educentric boxes and education's entrenched instructional assembly line will have your learners boasting about you for decades—and telling their children in future decades that they were pioneers in the noble effort that elevated education to its rightful place in their continuing age of empowerment.

EPILOGUE: LEARNING IN
THE AGE OF EMPOWERMENT

Congratulations to those of you who have shared with us the excitement of moving well beyond the conventional thinking of our era to explore what it might mean to educate in the age of empowerment—especially in a public system.

We've done our best to persuade you to expand your view of what education could look like if it were not the captive of institutional, legal, and cultural inertia—an inertia that powerful political forces in our society simply promote, legitimate, and reinforce, "reform" after "reform," decade after decade. And we've done it through examples of what real people in the real world have done and are doing that can readily be brought into the world's classrooms if those who control and those who operate in "the system" would agree to do so. But so far they haven't—mainly, we suspect, because they've chosen to remain in the comfort zone of the educentric boxes rather than explore (and implement) what lies beyond them.

Our best hope is that you—the "lead learner" in your organization—and countless colleagues like you, will bring the frameworks, thinking, examples, design strategies, vision, and logic that we've presented here to their attention. In doing so you'll be stepping into the role of also being the "lead teacher," a role that will clearly mark you as the "total professional" we described in *Total Leaders 2.0* and here in chapter 2—an identity that you'll carry with pride and continue to strengthen throughout your career. And you'll individually and collectively be expressing your own empowerment at a time that the world is crying for caring, enlightened exemplars.

As you move into this inspiring and challenging professional role, we'd like to offer you our "biggest picture" perspective on where we've been in this book, but also where we still could walk along the "learning in the age of empowerment" path. Note the difference between what we just said and the subtitle of this book. The latter is "educating in the age of empowerment," and we've certainly offered a variety of outside-the-box possibilities about it, with one of the key elements in our argument being that learning itself is inherently just that—*outside* the box.

You now recognize that, more than ever, modern societies are dragging, cramming, and forcing this huge unbounded phenomenon called learning into the narrow constraining boxes it calls "education." Along with it, of course, they're also dragging equally expansive concepts like achievement, accomplishment, competence, capacity, talent, intelligence, potential, results, and outcomes into the same narrow cells. If they do this long enough and with enough media reinforcement, they'll have almost every "modern" person on the planet believing that the education system's artificially constrained definitions of learning, achievement, et cetera, et cetera, are the only ones that matter. No, worse yet, make that, "the only ones that exist"!

So we're going to conclude by sharing with you a framework we developed in 2003. Actually, it's been the motivation for this book and all the things we've shared, but we haven't really shown you all of it. We laid the groundwork for it in chapters 1 and 3 and hinted at it more in chapters 4 and 5, but we didn't walk all the way down the "learning in the age of empowerment" path with you in our earlier chapters. But now we will, and it's what we'd really like you to take forward into your life and work.

Five Paradigms of Education

Let's just imagine that human civilization has historically offered us five different ways of approaching both learning and education. And let's further imagine that these five paradigms can be arrayed along a continuum. You can think of this as a ladder, a pathway, a mountain, or even a teeter-totter, and lay it out along either a vertical or horizontal axis if you wish. At one end of the continuum you have things that embody a distinctive set of characteristics, and at the other is a distinctly contrasting set. The closer you move to one pole or the other, the more the nature of its characteristics influences what's happening, and the weaker the other set becomes. Here's how that continuum looks to us:

Academic Standards	Performance Based	Life Performance	Personal Empowerment	Inner Realization

At one end of the continuum lies an approach to both education and learning that stresses the transmission and acquisition of culturally accepted knowledge. We call it the academic standards paradigm. Its "locus of control" for what is learned, by whom, and when, lies with the system and is external to the learner. In other words, the system calls the shots and characteristically operates in a masculine, hierarchical, linear way, with "IQ" being the capacity/ability that is honored and fostered the most. Its dominant instructional approach is direct instruction, its ethos is competitive, its rewards are externally determined, and its measures of success are virtually all quantitative—expressed as numerical grades, test scores, averages, and rankings.

At the other end of the continuum lies a paradigm that we have yet to describe and explore here. We call it inner realization. It invites the continuous, unbounded exploration, internalization, and expression of new and emerging experiences and possibilities. From these experiences, personal meaning, relevance, significance, and fulfillment emerge. Its essence is "human consciousness" and awareness, and it's manifested through the unique, personal, subjective expression of what we call personal identity and the human spirit.

As its name implies, the locus of control for what is experienced and learned lies wholly within the individual. Its key elements are curiosity, perception, intuition, and feeling, and the only conventional terms for instructional approaches that resonate with it are "guide," "facilitate," "model," and "mentor." And hardly any of it can be measured using conventional forms of testing, assessment, and demonstration. It is internal experience!

As you might imagine, formalized systems of whatever kind just don't connect with or foster this kind of deep, subjective human experience— even though inner realization is at least as relevant as academic content and performance to shaping who we are as humans, what we become, and how we relate and contribute to the world. As the two of us assessed the cultural and political climate and "realities" of this decade, we sincerely felt that the contrast and disconnect between the two poles of this continuum were just too great for educators to accommodate—not necessarily personally but organizationally. Hence, we chose not to go this far down the continuum in exploring what "public" ELCs would actually be allowed to address or do in the name of personalized, identity-shaping, learner-centered education.

What we felt comfortable doing, however, was to start across that continuum by embracing genuine performance-based models of various kinds. This was definitely a move in the learner empowerment direction, since it made real competence and the ability to do tangible things at least as important as knowing and remembering things in the conventional curriculum content boxes. In addition, this second paradigm challenges the sanctity of IQ as the only kind of ability that counts, and it dramatically strengthens the significance of doing, performing, creating, and implementing in the educational process.

We also felt confident in taking yet another step across the continuum in advocating the life performance template for defining learning outcomes for two compelling reasons. First, it enables educators for the first time to view and express learning in "human" terms—as people (of any age) with positive attributes—rather than as kinds of knowledge and skills in the abstract. Second, it is a powerful and persuasive link to being future focused and to connecting education to the challenges and opportunities of life in the age of empowerment.

Moving to this third paradigm, as you recall, also enabled us to see learning as a three-dimensional experience: (1) content and concepts, (2) applied competence, and (3) learning and performance contexts/settings. Once we had reached this balance point on the continuum, we were dealing heavily with "learners really matter" issues and dynamics. This new focus was reinforced by life-performance outcomes frameworks stressing self-direction, initiative, resourcefulness, teamwork, and productivity. Frameworks such as these literally impelled us to move forward to the next place on the continuum, personal empowerment.

We interpreted personal empowerment to be largely an expression of the unique talents and interests of individual learners. At this point on the continuum the locus of control clearly moves to the individual, the motivation for learning is intrinsic, the range of what can be learned expands radically, and the traditional notions of standardization and requirements significantly lose their relevance and power. This is where in chapter 6 we could begin to see that the possibility of learning in the age of empowerment as we described it in chapter 1 really become feasible for ELCs:

> Anyone can learn anything at anytime from anywhere from world-class experts using the most transformational technologies and resources available to enhance their personal interests and life fulfillment.

To us this statement means "The sky's the limit!" and that's where we began to rein in our vision of this book. Why? Because formal systems inherently limit the options open to their members, and the sky really isn't the limit for any of them, including NASA. Moreover, we just couldn't visualize the political and inertial forces at work in today's world allowing publicly supported education systems to address and implement inner realization, except incidentally, informally, and at the extreme periphery of their curricular offerings.

So that left us with the alternative of providing the best description we could of an incomplete journey toward an outcome called educational transformation—one that excludes inner realization, the final limitless leg being taken by millions of adults seeking deeper meaning and fulfillment in their lives.

As we noted in chapter 2 of *TL2.0*, this empowering leg of the journey is being fostered and facilitated by people with celebrity status such as Oprah Winfrey, Anthony Robbins, Wayne Dyer, Eckhart Tolle, the Dalai Lama, and Deepak Chopra. It's an exploration of our deepest essence as human beings, into the domain many call "spiritual," and it's one of the significant trends shaping the age of empowerment. And while the word "spiritual" conjures up massive confusion and resistance in many quarters, those on this ever-expanding leg of the journey realize that it has almost nothing to do with the endorsement or practice of "religion"—which is a key reason for the resistance.

So our biggest-picture view of "educating in the age of empowerment" comes down to three key things. First, with your participation and assistance these millions of people will eventually prevail. Those invested in educational change will begin the journey across the continuum of possibilities that we've taken together in this book because: (1) initiatives like EdVisions and the Adopting Communities for Excellence (ACE) program (where deep human development is seamlessly infused into both the main academic streams and the community partnerships that advance life-performance learning) will continue to expand their outreach, impact, and visibility; and (2) enlightened, empowered parents will demand them. Second, the resulting model will embrace and embody the strongest features and most empowering aspects of *all five* paradigms. Third, there will be dancing in the streets and playgrounds of the world's ELCs because humanity will finally have an educational system that is in harmony and balance with itself, with learners of all ages learning and living consciously, creatively, collaboratively, competently, and compassionately.

Oh yes, and the two of us can begin work on our next book: *Learning Communities 3.0: Educating in the Second Age of Enlightenment*!

SUPPORTING RESOURCES

Barker, J. (1988). *Discovering the Future: The Business of Paradigms*. St. Paul, MN: ILI Press.

Beck, D., and C. Cowan. (1996). *Spiral Dynamics*. Malden, MA: Blackwell.

Blanchard, K., and J. Britt. (2009). *Who Killed Change?* New York: HarperCollins.

Blanchard, K., and N. V. Peale. (1988). *The Power of Ethical Management*. New York: Morrow.

Blanchard, K., and G. Ridge. (2009). *Helping People Win at Work*. Upper Saddle River, NJ: FT Press.

Bolman, L. G., and T. E. Deal. (2001). *Leading with Soul: An Uncommon Journey of Spirit*. San Francisco: Jossey-Bass.

Brady, M. (2008). *Connections: Investigating Reality: A Course of Study* (formerly *Investigating Systems*). www.marionbrady.com.

Buckingham, M. (2005). *The One Thing You Need to Know about Great Managing, Great Leading, and Sustained Individual Success*. New York: Free Press.

Buckingham, M., and D. Clifton. (2001). *Now, Discover Your Strengths*. New York: Free Press.

Caine, G., and R. N. Caine. (2001). *The Brain, Education, and the Competitive Edge*. Lanham, MD: Rowman & Littlefield Education.

Caine, R. N., and G. Caine. (1991). *Making Connections: Teaching and the Human Brain*. Menlo Park, CA: Addison-Wesley.

———. (1997). *Education on the Edge of Possibility*. Alexandria, VA: Association for Supervision and Curriculum Development.

———. (1997). *Unleashing the Power of Perceptual Change*. Alexandria, VA: Association for Supervision and Curriculum Development.

Caine, R. N., G. Caine, C. McClintic, and K. Klimek. (2009). *Twelve Brain/ Mind Learning Principles in Action*. Thousand Oaks, CA: Corwin Press.

Carter, S. (1996). *Integrity*. New York: HarperCollins.

Collins, J. (2001). *Good to Great*. New York: HarperCollins.

Covey, S. R. (1989). *The Seven Habits of Highly Effective People*. New York: Simon & Schuster.

Damasio, A. (1999). *The Feeling of What Happens*. New York: Harcourt Brace.

Deal, T., and A. Kennedy. (1982). *Corporate Cultures*. New York: Perseus.

———. (2000). *The New Corporate Cultures*. New York: Perseus.

Engle, A. (2009). *Seeds of Tomorrow: Solutions for Improving Our Children's Education*. Boulder, CO: Paradigm Publishers.

Erickson, H. L. (2001). *Stirring the Head, Heart, and Soul: Redefining Curriculum and Instruction*. Thousand Oaks, CA: Corwin Press.

Fielding, M. (2000). The Person Centered School. *Forum, 42*(2), 51–54.

Fogarty, R. (1997). *Brain-Compatible Classrooms*. Arlington Heights, IL: Skylight Professional Development.

Gardner, H. (2004). *Changing Minds*. Boston: Harvard Business School Press.

———. (2006). *Five Minds for the Future*. Boston: Harvard Business School Press.

Goleman, D. (1995). *Emotional Intelligence*. New York: Bantam Books.

———. (2006). *Social Intelligence*. New York: Bantam Dell.

———. (2009). *Ecological Intelligence*. New York: Random House.

Goleman, D., R. Boyatzis, and A. McKee. (2002). *Primal Leadership*. Boston: Harvard Business School Press.

Hannaford, C. (2002). *Awakening the Child Heart*. Captain Cook, HI: Jamilla Nur Publishing.

Hicks, E., and J. Hicks. (2006). *The Amazing Power of Deliberate Intent*. Carlsbad, CA: Hay House.

Iacoboni, M. (2008). *Mirroring People: The New Science of How We Connect with Others*. New York: Farrar, Straus & Giroux.

Jensen, E. (1998). *Teaching with the Brain in Mind*. Alexandria, VA: Association for Supervision and Curriculum Development.

———. (2000). *Different Brains, Different Learners*. San Diego: The Brain Store.

Kelly, F. S., T. McCain, and I. Jukes. (2009). *Teaching the Digital Generation*. Thousand Oaks, CA: Corwin Press.

Kessler, R. (2000). *The Soul of Education*. Alexandria, VA: Association for Supervision and Curriculum Development.

Kohn, A. (1993). *Punished by Rewards*. Boston: Houghton Mifflin.

———. (1996). *Beyond Discipline: From Compliance to Community*. Alexandria, VA: Association for Supervision and Curriculum Development.

Labovitz, G., and V. Rosansky. (1997). *The Power of Alignment*. New York: Wiley.

Lambert, N., and B. L. McCombs. (1998). *How Students Learn: Reforming Schools through Learner-Centered Education*. Washington, DC: APA Books.

LeDoux, J. (1996). *The Emotional Brain*. New York: Simon & Schuster.

McCombs, B. L., and J. S. Whisler. (1997). *The Learner-Centered Classroom and School*. San Francisco: Jossey-Bass.

Miller, J. P. (1993). Worldviews, educational orientations, and holistic education. In R. Miller (Ed.), *The Renewal of Meaning in Education*. Brandon, VT: Holistic Education Press.

Montessori, M. (1966). *The Discovery of the Child*. Madras, India: Kalakshetra Publications.

———. (1967). *The Absorbent Mind*. Madras, India: Kalakshetra Publications.

Newell, R. J. (2003). *Passion for Learning*. Lanham, MD: Rowman & Littlefield Education.

Newell, R. J., and M. J. Van Ryzin. (2008). *Assessing What Really Matters in Schools*. Lanham, MD: Rowman & Littlefield Education.

Palfrey, J., and U. Glasser. (2008). *Born Digital*. New York: Basic Books.

Pert, C. B. (1997). *Molecules of Emotion*. New York: Scribner.

Pink, D. (2005). *A Whole New Mind*. New York: Riverhead Books.

———. (2009). *Drive*. New York: Riverhead Books.

Poscente, V. (2008). *The Age of Speed*. Austin, TX: Bard Press.

Posner, R. (2009). *Lives of Passion, School of Hope*. Boulder, CO: Sentient Publications.

Schlechty, P. C. (2002). *Inventing Better Schools*. San Francisco: Jossey-Bass.

Schwahn, C. J. (1993). *Making Change Happen: An Action-Planning Handbook*. Dillon, CO: Breakthrough Learning Systems.

Schwahn, C. J., and W. G. Spady. (2010). *Total Leaders 2.0*. Lanham, MD: Rowman & Littlefield Education.

Scott, S. (2002). *Fierce Conversations*. New York: Penguin.

Shirky, C. (2008). *Here Comes Everybody*. New York: Penguin.

Siegel, D. J. (1999). *The Developing Mind: Toward a Neurobiology of Interpersonal Experience*. New York: Guilford Press.

Spady, W. G. (1994). *Outcome-Based Education: Critical Issues and Answers*. Arlington, VA: American Association of School Administrators.

———. (1998). *Paradigm Lost: Reclaiming America's Educational Future*. Arlington, VA: American Association of School Administrators.

———. (2001). *Beyond Counterfeit Reforms*. Lanham, MD.: Scarecrow Press.

———. (2004). Using the SAQA critical outcomes to empower learners and transform education. *Perspectives in Education, 22*(2), 165–77.

———. (2007). The paradigm trap: Getting beyond the "No Child Left Behind" policy. *Education Week*, *26*(18), 27–29.

Stoddard, L. (2008). *Educating for Human Greatness*. Brandon, VT: Holistic Education Press.

Sylwester, R. (2000). *A Biological Brain in a Cultural Classroom*. Thousand Oaks, CA: Corwin Press.

Tapscott, D. (2009). *Grown Up Digital*. New York: McGraw-Hill.

Tapscott, D., and A. Williams. (2006). *Wikinomics: How Mass Collaboration Changes Everything*. London: Penguin.

Theobald, R. (1987). *The Rapids of Change*. Indianapolis, IN: Knowledge Systems.

Weinberger, D. (2007). *Everything Is Miscellaneous*. New York: Times Books.

Wilber, K. (2000). *A Theory of Everything*. Boston: Shambhala.

Zimmerman, B. J., and D. H. Schunk (Eds.). (2001). *Self-Regulated Learning and Academic Achievement* (2nd ed.). Mahwah, NJ: Erlbaum.

ABOUT THE AUTHORS

William G. Spady is the author of seven books and an internationally recognized authority on future-focused approaches to Outcome-Based Education, organizational change, transformational leadership development, strategic organizational design, and empowering models of learning and living. For more than forty years he has spearheaded major efforts throughout North America, South Africa, and Australia on expanding the vision, deepening the philosophical grounding, and improving the performance of educators, leaders, educational systems, and learners of all ages in business and the public sector. He loves classical music, skiing, bicycling, scuba diving, walking in nature, and reading anything that expands his awareness and deepens his spirituality. He can be reached at billspady@earthlink.net.

Charles J. Schwahn has made his professional life a study of leadership and effective organizations. For the past thirty years he has worked with businesses and school systems throughout North America providing consultation on the topics of leadership, change, and future-focused strategic design. His career has placed him in nearly all of the critical roles of the education profession, and his last "real" job was as superintendent of the Eagle County School District in Vail, Colorado. Chuck received his doctorate from the University of Massachusetts where Ken Blanchard of *The One-Minute Manager* fame, was his doctoral chair. Chuck and his wife Genny spend their summers in the Black Hills of South Dakota and winters in the Phoenix area. He can be reached at chuckschwahn@yahoo .com.